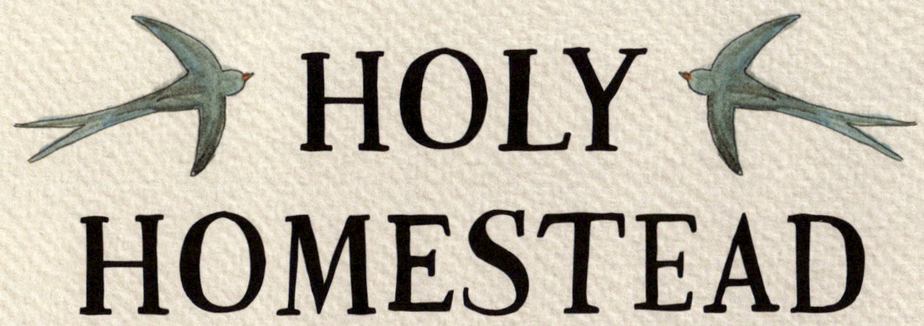

HOLY HOMESTEAD

A 6-Week Guide to Building a Faith-Filled, Sustainable Life

HANNAH DEURLOO

New York, New York

Good Books books may be purchased in bulk at special discounts for sales promotion, corporate gifts, fund-raising, or educational purposes. Special editions can also be created to specifications. For details, contact the Special Sales Department, Good Books, 307 Fifth Avenue, 4th Floor, New York, NY 10016.

Good Books is an imprint of Skyhorse Publishing, Inc.®, a Delaware corporation.

Visit our website at www.goodbooks.com.

10 9 8 7 6 5 4 3 2 1

Library of Congress Cataloging-in-Publication Data is available on file.

Cover design by Kai Texel
Cover and interior art by Hannah Deurloo
Interior design by Chris Schultz

Print ISBN: 978-1-964219-17-2
Ebook ISBN: 978-1-964219-29-5

Printed in China

DEDICATION:

For Our Home

Of all the things we learned from Covid, the most significant lesson was a new appreciation for our homes. Being at home could be enjoyable on a new level if we chose to make it so. Many of us picked up gardening, baking sourdough bread, crafting, and maybe a few chickens too. We invested in books, home offices, and backyard toys. Now most of us look forward to returning home at the end of a long day away because we have transformed our spaces into retreats. This book is dedicated to the home movement in all its unique ways—but especially to those seeking a homestead lifestyle with Jesus at its heart.

N
W
E
S

Contents

Carnations

Holy Homestead

Blessed

Introduction

You don't need a lot of land, or any at all, to live more sustainably. You don't even need a garden. Anyone can make small daily choices to live simply and do more at home. God has charged us to care for the Earth, which may mean making little changes in the things we do each day. We can all make incremental changes over time. This is not an insta-life. It will take time and work, but it's worth it.

In this book you will learn how to set up a homestead—how to make the most of your soil, land, and geographic location to get the best results for your family. You'll also find tips for the inner workings of your home—how to cook, preserve, and monetize your homestead. This book won't teach you everything you need to know to be a homesteader, but it will give you the framework to make the most of the gifts God has blessed you with. Let's walk together and build a plan for your family homestead.

Proverbs 31 does a deep dive into what a woman of God looks like. The passage is often called "the virtuous wife." I have a confession; I've never liked these verses. My husband has a tally of how many sad Mother's Day sermons I've listened to about how I don't measure up. But I re-read it this spring and it hit me like a sprinkler in the face—this virtuous wife was a *homesteader*. It wasn't that she was doing everything—it was that she was doing the best things for her family and home. Notice how her focus is on making yarn and weaving? She didn't also try to keep bees and make wine (yes, you can make wine at home, and it's actually super easy). She had a focus. That sprinkler is still soaking me here because I realized to my core, I have no focus. I want to do it all. But the reality is that I can't do it all.

But what *can* I do? This book will help you figure out where your focus should be based on where you live, what your skills are, and your time parameters. But before we begin, it's important to remember the main focus will always be to glorify God. If at any point you find yourself focusing on fear, comparison, anger, pride, or have lost peace in your heart, it's time to stop and refocus on God. Just like any good gift in life, Satan has a plan to turn it into a stumbling stone in our walk with God. Be on your guard for this, it will happen, and it may be happening now. Take the next ten minutes to pray and be still before God, ask Him to lead you in this process.

If you're wondering if God cares if you plant extra zucchini or sunflowers, *He does*! God cares about every facet of our lives. Walk through your home and give each space to God and His plan. Walk through your yard, garden, and garage and tell God you want to glorify Him and work for His kingdom plans. Get your family onboard with the idea that everything we are and own is God's and we should be stewarding with God's will in mind.

Also know that this process of making our homesteads and our lives grow with God is not fast or easy. It's hard work. But God wants us to work; before the fall, God called work "good." God's perfect plan is coming to fruition in Jesus, and we need only ask Him to guide us as we seek to honor God in our homes and lives. So, grab your metaphorical muck boots and sunhat and dig in—this here is good work.

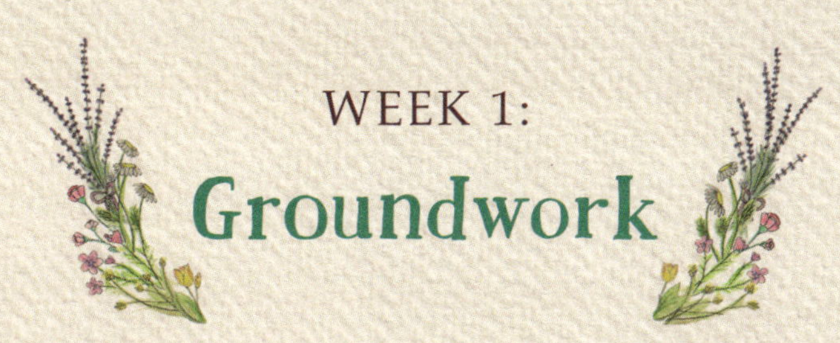

WEEK 1: Groundwork

One time while out walking with my kids, we stumbled upon an epic patch of wild blackberries (we call them blackcaps in our area). We picked and picked and picked. I told the girls we'd go home and make yummy jam ("yummy" is the technical term at my house for delicious). They helped me clean the berries and cook them, but as we added the sugar, I realized my stash of pectin powder was gone. I needed to improvise or else we'd miss out on yummy jam!

My backup thickener is lemon juice. Alas, we had no lemons either, *but* we did have an orange. *Close enough*, I thought. Unfortunately, it was not close enough; our jam did not set. Thankfully, my kids didn't care if the berry concoction was thick or runny and they happily ate it up. My kids are full of grace, and often I am not. I was upset with myself, at what felt like a "failure."

Have you ever started a project or recipe only to discover you are missing a part or item you need to finish well? I should have taken inventory of what ingredients I had first before starting the project. At the end of Luke 14 in verses 25–33, Jesus gives several parables about taking stock of where you are before jumping into things. He explains that starting a building project or anything without first counting the cost is foolish. Jesus is so right in this—not only should we think about the material aspects of this lifestyle, but we should also take stock of the spiritual realities.

Have you counted the cost for Jesus? He asks us to surrender our lives, homes, money—everything—to Him. In 1 Peter 2:7 it says, "Yes, you who trust [Jesus] recognize the honor God has given him. But for those who reject him, 'The stone that the builders rejected has now become the cornerstone'" (NLT). Jesus is the "cornerstone." In a building, a cornerstone is the place a structure begins, its foundation, and everything is upheld by that one block—it's more than a big deal. The cornerstone makes everything stand or fall and everything is measured from it. So first, before we begin this journey, let's ask Jesus what He wants to use our homes for. Request that He remove fear of the future and failure. Beseech Jesus for wisdom as you work through this for you and your family. In Proverbs 31:16 the woman "considers a field" before buying it. Let's take a step back and consider what about your home brings glory to God.

Day 1: Compass Points

I have a geography quiz for you. If you are standing at your front door, which way is North? Take a moment to figure this out (if you need help, your phone probably has an app that can tell you). Whether you want to grow things inside or out, knowing your compass is a big deal. It's where we are going to start.

Imagine this aerial drawing is your home (I know your home may not be this exact shape but let us pretend). Now fill in the compass points as they are at your home. Got it? Great! You're laying solid groundwork for your homestead.

Next, add trees if you have any. Think about how big the shadows of your trees are (or your neighbor's trees, or adjacent building shade). Add in your trees to the drawing using a circle or fluffy cloud shape. Gardens—and even most houseplants—usually grow best in full sun on the south side of your home or property. (We will assume you do not live in a desert climate, but if you do, utilizing the north side for gardening would be best because it will keep your plants cooler.)

Go back to the house drawing and place a square near the south side of your home in an area that has full sun (six or more hours of sunshine per day). If the south side is not an option, then the next best choice is the west side because it utilizes the evening heat best, and then the next best choice is the east side to get morning sunshine. This square is the best location for your garden geographically.

But wait!

What if the best spot for the garden is the front yard? Do you really want to be doing your gardening out front where all the neighbors can watch? That's exactly what happened at my house. My garden is right on the corner of our lot with the road on two sides. While it took a little bit of time to convince my husband, overall, it has been the best choice not only for my garden productivity but also for being neighborly. My neighbors walk by and I'm there in the garden, so I say hello. If you say hello enough, they may ask a question. It may lead to a conversation. It may even lead to prayer. What an amazing opportunity! My garden has become a Jesus zone by being in a visible area where my neighbors can see me.

But what if you have no outdoor space? There may be options in the community; churches and cities often have allotments to rent or for free. Or maybe you have a friend with a yard, and you decide to make a garden together and share the responsibilities and harvests. This is another way to build a community around homesteading. You do not have to do this alone.

Even a window herb garden is a great way to start. My go-to herbs I cook with are basil, rosemary, thyme, peppermint, and sage. You can plant them in a single long planter or put each in its own cute jar to keep around the kitchen for easy cooking. Again, use your compass points to locate a sunny south window if you can.

The Bible talks about compass points, too. Psalm 103:12 says, "He has removed our sins as far from us as the east is from the west" (NLT). What an amazingly immeasurable distance! Praise the Lord! Be still before Jesus for five minutes thinking about the joy and freedom from sin we have in Him. Thank God for His great kindness.

If you're already looking at your home on paper and your mind is spinning because there's "no room," or if you worry about "adding on" or whatever it is, just wait. All these ideas have a place, but sometimes the excitement gets ahead of us. When my husband and I first got married we bought a fixer-upper, and I don't mean a cute one that needed "updates." It needed to be gutted to the studs, and with each layer we uncovered more issues. Those were some of the hardest years of our marriage. If you're married or undertaking a project in partnership with someone else, take some time to figure out your goals and desires together before jumping into anything. Weigh your dreams against your resources and abilities so you don't bite off more than you can chew.

To do: Use a piece of graph paper to chart your home and land, add the compass points, shade zones, and other features you feel are important (like hose spigots and driveways). Make a few copies to use later in this book.

Day 2: Layout

The second chapter of Luke holds a beautiful example of repurposing. A brand-new mother and father look around at the place that God has placed them. They need to lay their baby in a safe place, a place they would never have planned to be themselves. Mary and Joseph were in a stable, probably a cave cut into limestone rock, a place for animals. Baby Jesus was here, on Earth, Emmanuel! But where could they lay him down? There was no snuggly bed. No grandparents to hand him off to when they needed a break. They were far from their support network.

They laid Jesus in a manger, where animals eat. A humble beginning for the Son of God! I don't know about you, but I would not have wanted that for my child. I would've wanted the first-century equivalent of a special bedroom with perfect matching crib, adorable nightlights twinkling overhead. But Mary and Joseph used what God provided. I confess I tend to chase the ideal. I want the best. But that's not always what God has planned.

Often God wants us to look around at the place He has put us and say, "Okay, it's not what I would have picked, God, but what is here that I'm not seeing?" He wants us to be still for a little while and ask again, "God, give me your eyes for my home and yard so I can see the potential and not only what's missing."

Take a few moments and pray those lines above. Let yourself think about the spaces inside and around your home. Consider what is underutilized—maybe the "catch-all" space that has never quite found its purpose. Now think about what your family needs to function better. Is it a place to put all the shoes, a desk to organize the bills, or a space to store all the canned garden goods? The need will be unique to your family and there are no wrong answers.

Matthew 6:8 says, ". . . For your Father knows the things you have need of before you ask Him." What if we lived like this statement was true? What if we believed that God has anticipated and knows all our needs and is already meeting them? I don't know if Mary waddled into that stable and saw the manger and said to Joseph, "Oh, good place to lay Jesus." More likely, she laid down in a pile of hay and prayed, "God, I don't understand, but I trust you will provide."

We should expect God to show up and have a plan. It may not be our plan, but His plans are always better. Look at your home and property with new eyes, look and see what God has already provided. Try to see His plan or provision in a way you hadn't considered before. Pray for eyes to see it.

What about those of us who value the traditional American lawn? The pristine grass cut at all the right angles with no dandelions in sight, the "keeping up with the Jones's" look? I would challenge you to consider where your heart is. Lawns are not bad, but if they are used as a status symbol and for comparison, then they can be a stumbling block. Maybe God has something else in mind for your lawn.

Be careful of Satan and his capacity to take something good and twist our hearts around it like a prize above all else. If you start a homestead, the lawn will likely take a hit because gardens are messy, chickens make noise, and compost smells bad. You will have to come to terms with these things.

I should also say, if your lawn is immaculate and you want to keep all of it that way, then still find a way to bring glory to God through it. Maybe you host a fundraiser on the lawn or use it to gather your community for a barbeque Bible study! Just be sure to keep Jesus at the core. Use it for God's glory, not your own.

I grew up playing the Oregon Trail game on my family computer during the long winter days. It was fun to plan out supplies and try to barter and hunt, but I almost never made it to the end of the trail. I would restart again and try one more time to avoid being sunk in the river or getting typhoid or starving. What I didn't grasp at the time was the extreme perseverance of those that did legitimately travel that broken road out West. They were looking for a future to believe in and to work for. We have so much available to us compared to what the early homesteaders had to make do with. Most of us will never live more than an hour's drive from a grocery store. But still, any form of homesteading requires perseverance. It's not about stockpiling all the supplies you might need or thinking ahead to every possible obstacle—it's about taking one step at a time with faith and intentionality.

To do: Measure and sketch out your underutilized home or yard space. Is it a closet or a section of lawn or a basement corner? Now imagine how it could meet a need for your family. Make multiple ideas come to life on paper as you dream. Notice how God may be providing for you in ways you hadn't considered before. If you're feeling stuck, browse Pinterest for inspiration.

Day 3: Time Management & Preparedness

Be Choosy

Statistically, most families that start homesteading quit within seven years. I want you to defy this statistic. The best way to make sure you can maintain this way of living is to start with intentional incremental steps. For example, if someone offers you a free rabbit and you've never considered rabbits before, say, "Thanks, but I'll need to put some thought into this." Go home and do your research, look at what a rabbit needs to live well, what different varieties are bred for, and consider whether raising rabbits is the best use of your time (see chapter Week 5 for more information on animals). Maybe it is! But don't let the fear of missing out make you say yes before you're ready for a new commitment. Once you are prepared, saying "Yes!" will become a blessing instead of a struggle.

God has the best timing every time. Ecclesiastes 3 is a long list of all the "times" that God has planned in our lives. Some are exciting and some are not, but what God is getting at is that we should "enjoy the good of all our labor" (verse 13) as it is a "gift of God." How encouraging that we can find contentment in each moment of life regardless of what is happening.

Be Intentional

I encourage you to find a routine and develop habits as you work through this book that allow you to serve your family and home best. Instead of getting to the end of the day and realizing you still have loads on your to-do list, be intentional with your time. Here is an easy way to break down your homesteading tasks throughout the day:

	Garden Chores	Animal Chores	Kitchen Chores	Family Needs
Morning				
Afternoon				
Evening				

Be Prepared

Lately, with all the disasters in the news, I've had to rethink some of our emergency plans for our homestead. What would happen if we lost power for days? What if the heat stopped in the middle of winter? Am I certain God would provide? Yes, I believe He would. But He has also taught me how to prepare and be ready. Think about what your unique needs would be in the event of a natural disaster, power outage, or supply chain disruption. These are a few preparedness tools that you can have on hand for when things get extreme:

- Generator, chainsaw, bottled water, emergency plan, and extra blankets.
- What would you add for your home and area? ....
  ....

Learn how your house works so that emergencies don't hit so hard. Things like:

- Where are the best exits for your home? Teach your kids, too.
- How do you shut off your water at the source (like under sinks, toilets, etc.)?
- Where are your electrical breakers to shut off power to your home?
- What's your plan if power does fail for more than 24 hours?

It's also important to note that anticipating every possible disaster is not the point. When we try to do too much, we overwhelm ourselves and disregard the seasons that God has set up in our lives. Ecclesiastes 3:11 says, "He has made everything beautiful in its time." When we seek to do anything outside of its time, it does not work the way God intends. Take a few minutes to pray over the season God has your family in right now. Ask God what things you are forcing into season and what things are blooming that you may be missing. Pray for a clear focus in this next year so you don't overextend your family.

Be Realistic

Your garden will not be "Instagram worthy" the first few years. It will be functional, at best. Your sourdough will flop sometimes, and those ingredients will be wasted. Your animals will die at some point, and it will be hard. Over time, you will grow in experience, and things will get easier. Keep reminding yourself of Ecclesiastes 3 and how it all adds up to a full year of seasons in God's hands and plans.

You will need to try and fail in this homesteading lifestyle to succeed over time. This is why I recommend starting small and with things that will directly benefit your family so you can see the results right away in a positive way. Once you've got a good routine on your first goal, then move on to the next.

To start, think about what your family needs and likes the most. It could be sourdough bread, an herb garden, or laying hens. Does your family make smoothies each day? Then maybe you should plant a berry garden and focus on that. Do you love tea? If so, you can create an herb garden. Maybe you love fresh flowers and the joy they bring, in which case a flower garden may be what you should plant—and you can pass the joy of fresh flowers along to others, too! Do you love essential oils? You can plant an oils garden and invest in a distillery setup. Here are some breakdowns so you can think about where you want to invest your family's time:

- Sourdough breadmaking takes an active time of 30–60 minutes a day (apart from fermentation and baking time).
- Chickens take about 15 minutes a day to feed and care for them. Plus, seasonal coop cleanups that will take several hours.
- Depending on the season and size, a garden can take 10–30 minutes a day to maintain weeding and watering. Planting and harvesting adds more time.

Think about what resources you already have. For example, my parents have bees, so I can trade or buy from them and invest my time into something else. I also have a local bicycle trail that is lined with wild blackberries which are free to pick, so in my garden I choose to plant a different berry that I don't have easy foraging access to. It is good to have a journal with these resources listed out so you can easily reference them. I like to organize mine by season.

Remember, the times and seasons are all in God's hands and we can trust Him in that. Take five minutes to be still in joy and contentment for God's amazing ability to do it all when we can't.

To do: Ask your family what things they dream about doing with their time. Does your family want chickens, bees, a garden, or to learn skills like woodworking? These ideas can be practical, like providing food for your family, or for the joy of it, like making a dugout canoe from a log. Take a realistic look at the time requirements for these items, while also looking at your other time commitments. For example, are kids' sports overtaking family time altogether? What needs to be left behind in this season? Honor these answers in this current season. As things change and you enter new seasons, revisit these questions and pray that God guides your family.

Day 4: What You Already Have: Plant & Soil Identification

Plant Identification

A couple of days ago we talked about seeing your home with new eyes. Today we are going to look at what your home or property already has that could be useful. Many outdoor spaces have a selection of landscaping plants or garden beds you can utilize. One of the most overwhelming things can be just figuring out what plants you already have around your home. You can get plant identification books from your local library or join an online plant identification group to help you with this. I also have an app on my phone that I use to learn what's around my house and community.

Here are some plant terms you should know:

- **Variegated:** when the leaves have multiple colors like lime green, dark green, and white.
- **Evergreen:** a pine or cypress-type tree that does not drop leaves in the autumn.
- **Annual/biennial/perennial:** identifies how long a plant will live—one year, two years, or multiple years.
- **Hardiness zones:** geographic areas defined by temperatures, helping you determine which plants are likely to survive through the winter months.
- **Spacing:** how much room a plant needs to grow into a mature size.

Foraging was one of the things that got me started on my homestead journey, simply because I didn't have the land or time for much else. If that feels like you, then getting a foraging app is a great place to start as they can keep track of different plants and locations you've already identified and when you can return to harvest from them year after year.

Be aware that some land is not allowed to be harvested from, depending on your state laws. But it's often easy to find "free food" in your local area if you know what you're looking for. Some easy places to find "free" food include:

- Walking and biking trails
- Local parks and camping areas
- Cemeteries
- Edges of public baseball and soccer fields

Foraged foods include things like tree nuts, berries, medicinal "weeds," and mushrooms.

Soil Identification

Next let's look at your soil. This one is a big deal. Jesus talks about soils in Luke 8:4–15, the parable of the Sower. While many pastors preach on being the seed that grows in God, I want to talk for a moment about the actual dirt. Unless you're growing sprouts, then soil is essential, and not all dirt is the same. Jesus tells us that dirt that is rocky will cause a plant to not root well, soil that is too hard will cause seeds to shrivel or get eaten, and soil full of thorns will choke out a plant. But the good soil, that's where a harvest can happen. Jesus was talking to people who gardened. They knew what he was saying in a practical sense even if they missed the heart application.

So, what kind of soil do you have? Odds are it will need work. We all need to work on the soil of our hearts and in our yards. Let's take a moment to pray that God works our hearts into good soil that isn't choked by life's sins, or dryness from lack of community, or full of rocky pride. Ask God to fill you with grace, meekness, and joy as we dig deeper into this homesteading work.

Soil quality matters because the food you grow in it absorbs nutrients from the soil. Plants need enough nutrients to thrive, and produce grown in nutrient-rich soil contains higher amounts of vitamins and minerals. When dirt is depleted of its natural minerals and nutrients, it's referred to as "dead" and your produce will suffer in quality and, eventually, we as people do as well. There are a few different ways to approach the dirt in your yard. One way is to ignore it and simply add new dirt that you know is good. Another way is to amend the soil you have. Neither of these options are wrong and I would say that it depends on your resources.

- If you have raised garden beds or are planting inside, then buying good dirt is the way to go.
- If you are planting a garden, then tilling up the ground and adding compost to it makes sense.

What I like to do is a layered mulch garden so I can avoid extra equipment and weeding at my home. To decide what method is best for you, I would do a soil test and find out if you have acidic, neutral, or alkaline soil. Decide if you want that soil type or if you need to change it based on what you want to grow. For example, hydrangea flowers will be pink in soil that is alkaline 6.5 pH or higher and blue to purple in soil that is acidic 6 pH or less. Neutral is a pH of 7. At our house, part of my garden is acidic, and part is alkaline so I can grow a wider variety of plants. It all depends on your focus and needs as a family. Here is a short list of plants that like each soil type:

- **Highly acidic soil (4.5–5.5 pH):** Sweet potatoes, potatoes, cranberries, currants, peppers, rhubarb, raspberries, oregano, sage, blueberries, elderberries, foxgloves, zinnias, and daffodils.
- **Neutral soil (6–7 pH):** Many plants thrive here in the middle and it's ideal to aim for this for the best results.
- **Alkaline soil (7.1–8 pH):** Lavender, poppy, asparagus, leeks, parsnips, beets, and marjoram.

Going back to the parable of the sower, Jesus didn't talk about acidity, He talked about what the soil was made of, like sand, rocks, loam, and clay. Jesus isn't wrong—the texture of your dirt matters, too!

- **Sand:** Just like the sand at the beach, it's great for drainage but not for holding water on dry days. If you have too much sand, you can add clay or compost to start transforming it into good soil.
- **Rocks:** It's nearly impossible to grow in rocky soil. My home used to have a railroad track going right by it and the result has been gravel-like soil for us. To fix this, I've been adding layers of organic matter and letting it decompose into a new layer of loamy soil on top of the gravel. Another good option is raised garden beds and bringing in new dirt that is already balanced.

- **Clay:** Dense soil that is hard when dry and slimy when wet. Add sand and organic matter to change the consistency to a more workable soil.
- **Loam:** Ideal, fluffy soil that is dark in color, holds water well, and is rich in organic matter.

No matter what kind of soil you have, you can grow things in it for your family. I have learned to work with my soil by planting things which like the rocky, sandy mix we already have, like blueberries and asparagus. If this feels like too much to consider and your mind is humming with uncertainty, then take a deep breath. The answer can be as simple as container gardening where you don't have to question the soil type because you buy it already adjusted and ready to go.

It's also a good idea to test your water. This will tell you if your water has contaminants in it. Being near large agricultural fields means we have high nitrates in ours. Your water may be through the city and be treated with fluoride. Once you have learned about your water quality, you can choose to filter your water in a few ways:

- **Whole home systems:** Saltwater filters and reverse osmosis systems.
- **Faucet filters:** Attach directly to a faucet and use a small filter attachment.
- **Pitcher filters:** Filter is located in a water pitcher that filters as you pour.

Remember your plants, inside and outside, will want water that is not treated with fluoride or salt as those cause plants to die over time. So, consider where you fill up your watering can.

To do: Download a plant identification app on your phone. This will help you discern between plants that are useful and ones to be avoided (like poison ivy). Take a soil sample and decide if you need to amend your soil or keep it like it is. Get your water tested and consider if it needs adjustments. Pray and ask God if gardening is what He is calling you to do. Ask your family what they think about the option of a garden at your home.

Day 5: Not Buying Into It

I caught myself looking at the cutest view of a cozy farm on my laptop. If only my house looked like this, I thought, then I'd be happy. The chickens were red, the pond was lush, the grass was perfect . . . too perfect. I looked closer and realized there were no paths of travel in the grass and the blooming apple tree was next to a thriving pumpkin patch, which is seasonally impossible. This image had been generated by AI, and yet I had fallen for it. My heart was shallower than that AI-generated pond full of koi fish.

We all fall for the consumer mindset we've been raised in. If you want to make sourdough bread, then of course you "need" the big bread bowl, the specialized scoring knives, the perfect apron, and the vintage fermentation jar for your starter. But 1 Timothy 6 gives a warning not to live a life in pursuit of money and things. Verse 6 says, "Now godliness with contentment is great gain." Not that having money is wrong, but when money—instead of Jesus—becomes the goal, then we are in error.

Let me put it this way, do not let the desire (read: greed) for a highland cow, or a Victorian greenhouse, or a freeze dryer come between you and God. Take a moment to go to God in prayer and confess those items that have moved from the "dream" category to the "greed" category in our hearts and minds. Now ask God to guard your heart and mind from this ever-present temptation.

Take stock of what you do have for equipment. This can be things like shovels and rakes, a borrowed rototiller, a large kitchen for preserving, or maybe a shed you could convert into a chicken coop. Make a list below:

- Garden items: ....
  ....
- Animal care items: ....
  ....
- Preserving items: ....
  ....
- Other items: ....
  ....

Do you notice something about this list above? God has already greatly provided for you! Philippians 4:19 says, "And my God shall supply all your need according to His riches in glory by Christ Jesus." Paul is talking to a young church who has sent him money to help him while he is in jail. This church had just given up money and here Paul is testifying that God knows what they need and can supply it. This is not a prosperity promise for wealth and riches, it's a statement that God knows our needs and meets them. It may not be that we get a 40-acre farmhouse with a wraparound porch, but you do have a home, and the sun shines on it, and the sink brings you water to use. Don't take these blessings for granted.

It's hard for me to pass up a trip to the thrift store; maybe you can relate. Or do HomeGoods and Target sing a siren song from the decorative pillows section? Either way, let's talk about home décor for a little bit. Growing up, I watched my grandma decorate for each season with a passion I have only seen matched at department stores. She had a tote (or three) for each holiday and seeing her house all decked out was one of my highlights as a kid. Her joy was sharing holiday cheer and I think it was wonderful. I'm not nearly as dedicated as she was in her décor shifts, but I do have a bit of space dedicated to decorating "stuff" in our basement. As I pass those dusty shelves, I'm convicted that I have too much. I am not the master decorator that my grandma was—it's just not my priority—and I need to be choosy with what I keep so that I have space for what matters most in *our* home. Do you sometimes walk through your home and feel overwhelmed by the amount of stuff inside it? To help me with this, I have created a few questions I ask myself before I buy something:

1. Is it useful?
2. Is it beautiful?
3. Is there someone on my heart I can gift this to?
4. What can I remove from my home so that this has a spot?

5. Would this purchase honor our budget?

The bottom line is that the world says you need more (and more and more) to be content and happy. The truth is that you probably have enough stuff already to start homesteading today without even a trip to the hardware store (or to your Amazon account). If I'm being gut-wrenchingly honest, I wanted you to buy this book (thank you), but you probably could've looked online for free for much of this information. I'm praying that you walk away with more than a baby homestead. I pray you have a mind totally set on Jesus and how He can use your homestead for His glory as you learn and grow. So don't buy into the culture of more as you start this journey. Be scrappy. Be thrifty. Use things up. Wear things out. Flip a fence and make it a trellis. Whatever we really need, God provides, if only we have eyes to see it.

To do: Make a new list of all the equipment you want in your homestead—maybe it is even a new home. Write it all down. Now decide which of those things can be gotten in the short term, medium term, and long term. This is the beginning of your goals and dreams. Now look at the list you made on page 21 of items you already have. This is your "can start now" list. This is your action list for the coming months to begin moving toward a homestead lifestyle with the least amount of effort and money.

Equipment Wants	Under 3 Months	6+ Months	1+ Years

WEEK 2:
Gardening

We've made it to week two. Congratulations! You've done a lot of thinking and preparing up to this point. Hopefully, you've done even more praying about the direction your family should go with this process. This week we are going to dig deep into all things gardening. There are so many options in this category, and I am confident you will find the right way for your family. Even if you don't think you want to garden, please don't skip over this section as there are more ways to garden than just dirt in the backyard.

Before God made Adam and Eve in Genesis 2, He made a garden. God filled it with wonderful plants to eat, rivers to water it, and at least a couple of trees. We know how the tree part turned out, but before that, God told Adam in verse 15 to "tend and keep" the garden. What an amazing job—the first job. On day 8 of creation, God made a gardener. If God thought gardening would be a good first job for humanity, then we should at least consider it for ourselves. Pray that God teaches you His heart for gardening and the Earth. Ask Him for the desire to love and care for it in a way that fits you and your family.

I grew up with a garden just like my mom did. Neither of us appreciated it at first, but it didn't take long after having our families to see the value in it. I remember summers in the country going like this:

"Mom, I'm bored!"

"Go play outside, take your siblings with you."

We'd all file outside.

“Mom, I’m thirsty!”

“Drink out of the hose.”

It was cold and refreshing, which led to playing in the water, too.

“Mom, I’m hungry!”

“Eat out of the garden.”

We would run our bare feet through the dirt looking for green beans, raspberries, cucumbers, and sugary snap peas.

We’d get the call for dinner and come in tired and happy, take baths to clean the dirt off, and eat warm dinner rolls to fill us up before bed. I never knew those things were their own kind of medicine until looking back on them as an adult. It was fresh air, sunshine, vitamins, and earth between our toes. We played, we explored, we pretended, we sang, and we lived. If I can give any of these experiences to my kids, I will. I want my kids to associate a buzzing sound with a bumble bee and not with phone notifications. I want my kids to know how food comes to be and not just think it’s from the store. If you can relate, then let’s find a garden that’s right for you.

Day 1: Garden Types

When it comes to gardening, I am convinced there is a kind for everyone. From a traditional Native American controlled burn to improve berry production to the mechanical rototiller or the windowsill of herbs, there is something for us all. In Psalm 104, God talks about all the types of gardens He has planted near streams, in valleys, plants for people to enjoy, and trees that shelter the birds. Take a few minutes to read Psalm 104 and marvel at all He has made.

Psalm 104

Bless the Lord, O my soul!

O Lord my God, You are very great:
You are clothed with honor and majesty,
Who cover *Yourself* with light as *with* a garment,
Who stretch out the heavens like a curtain.

He lays the beams of His upper chambers in the waters,
Who makes the clouds His chariot,
Who walks on the wings of the wind,
Who makes His angels spirits,
His ministers a flame of fire.

You who laid the foundations of the earth,
So *that* it should not be moved forever,
You covered it with the deep as *with* a garment;
The waters stood above the mountains.
At Your rebuke they fled;
At the voice of Your thunder they hastened away.
They went up over the mountains;
They went down into the valleys,
To the place which You founded for them.

You have set a boundary that they may not pass over,
That they may not return to cover the earth.

He sends the springs into the valleys;
They flow among the hills.
They give drink to every beast of the field;
The wild donkeys quench their thirst.
By them the birds of the heavens have their home;
They sing among the branches.
He waters the hills from His upper chambers;
The earth is satisfied with the fruit of Your works.

He causes the grass to grow for the cattle,
And vegetation for the service of man,
That he may bring forth food from the earth,
And wine *that* makes glad the heart of man,
Oil to make *his* face shine,
And bread *which* strengthens man's heart.
The trees of the Lord are full *of sap,*
The cedars of Lebanon which He planted,
Where the birds make their nests;
The stork has her home in the fir trees.
The high hills *are* for the wild goats;
The cliffs are a refuge for the rock badgers.

He appointed the moon for seasons;
The sun knows its going down.
You make darkness, and it is night,
In which all the beasts of the forest creep about.
The young lions roar after their prey,
And seek their food from God.
When the sun rises, they gather together
And lie down in their dens.
Man goes out to his work
And to his labor until the evening.

O Lord, how manifold are Your works!
In wisdom You have made them all.
The earth is full of Your possessions—
This great and wide sea,
In which *are* innumerable teeming things,
Living things both small and great.
There the ships sail about;
There is that Leviathan
Which You have made to play there.

These all wait for You,
That You may give *them* their food in due season.
What You give them they gather in;
You open Your hand, they are filled with good.
You hide Your face, they are troubled;
You take away their breath, they die and return to their dust.
You send forth Your Spirit, they are created;
And You renew the face of the earth.

May the glory of the Lord endure forever;
May the Lord rejoice in His works.
He looks on the earth, and it trembles;
He touches the hills, and they smoke.

I will sing to the Lord as long as I live;
I will sing praise to my God while I have my being.
May my meditation be sweet to Him;
I will be glad in the Lord.
May sinners be consumed from the earth,
And the wicked be no more.

Bless the Lord, O my soul!
Praise the Lord!

Pray verse 31 reaches into your heart with joy: "May the glory of the LORD endure forever; May the LORD rejoice in His works." Did you catch it? God Himself rejoices in the Earth He has made. If God can find His glory reflected in nature, so can we.

Let's figure out what kind of gardening is best for your family. As you read through these options, make some notes on the ones that resonate with you.

For Our Family?	Ways to Garden	Equipment Needs	Difficulty Level	Average Time
	Tilled gardens are created by digging up your garden space (with a tractor, rototiller, or shovel) to prepare the soil for planting. Weeds need to be managed by weeding regularly, plastic ground covers, or weed killers. This is a common method for most gardens. You can grow anything that works for your soil and climate in this garden.	Medium to High	Moderate	30 min–1 hour per day for a 20' × 20' area
	Layered gardens are created by placing cardboard, leaves, straw, and/or woodchips over the garden area every year. This creates a weed prevention barrier and builds up the soil over time. Plants are then planted into the layers to grow. You can grow anything that works for your soil and climate in this garden.	Low to Medium	Easy	30 mins or less per day for a 20' × 20' area
	Raised garden beds are great at preventing small animals from eating your plants, or if you have difficulty being on your hands and knees in the garden. Beds are small enough to work up the soil with hand tools and weed as needed. You can grow anything that works for your soil and climate in this garden.	Medium	Moderate	10–30 min a day for a 4' × 8' space
	Greenhouse gardens are an amazing way to extend your garden season or to protect some plant varieties. You will have to monitor and maintain the climate inside the greenhouse for optimal plant health. This includes watering as rain will not reach inside the greenhouse.	Medium to High	Moderate to Hard	30 min–1 hour per day depending on what is planted

For Our Family?	Types of Gardens	Equipment Needs	Difficulty Level	Average Time
	Windowsill gardens are small indoor gardens that are only as big as the space you have available. Often, they are used for kitchen herbs or microgreens.	Low to Medium	Easy	10 min a day
	Forest gardens are specialized areas beneath tree cover that utilize the dappled shade and mimic the edge of a field in nature. Plants like berry bushes, climbing vines, mushrooms, and fruit trees thrive in this type of garden.	Low	Moderate	10–30 min per day for every 12 linear feet of tree line
	Cut flower gardens are beautiful and can be a great source of income. You can plant cut flowers in tilled, layered, or raised beds but each type of flower will have its own needs to be cut, deadheaded, and sometimes stored for winter.	Medium to High	Moderate to hard	30 min–1 hour per day depending on flower varieties planted
	Vegetable gardens are a great way to provide for your family or for your community. You can plant vegetables in any style garden that you prefer.	Medium	Moderate	15 min–1 hour per day
	Mushroom gardens are easy to start with some freshly cut tree limbs or in a five-gallon bucket of straw depending on what kind you want to grow. You will need either a cool space in your home or a shady spot outside to produce.	Low to Medium	Easy to Moderate	10 min or less per day
	Color gardens are created by selecting a color and focusing all your plantings within that color palette. This can range from purple peppers to pink celery or black sunflowers. There are many unique varieties of plants available. You can use the tilled, layered, or raised beds methods for this type of garden.	Medium	Moderate	10–30 min per day depending on plants and planting method used

(*Continued . . .*)

For Our Family?	Types of Gardens	Equipment Needs	Difficulty Level	Average Time
	Night gardens are curated by planting flowers and plants that bloom exclusively at night. They pair well with bat houses and star gazing. You can use the tilled, layered, or raised beds methods for this type of garden.	Medium	Moderate	10–30 min per day depending on plants and planting method used
	Rain gardens are specifically useful for areas that have regular amounts of high water like ditches, gullies, and swamps. There are many plants that thrive in these conditions and can handle the ebb and flow of water well. This method may also utilize rock features to catch and curb fast water flow, which will allow plants to thrive. Look for plants that like "wet feet" or "damp roots," like elderberry.	Medium	Medium to Hard	10–30 min per day
	Medicinal gardens are great for making tinctures, healing teas, and medicine. This pairs well with taking classes or learning in this area to support your growing. Goes well with mushroom gardening too.	Low	Medium to Hard	30 min per day prepping herbs for picking and then processing them correctly

Did you see a garden type or style that you fell in love with? Maybe two or three? You don't have to commit to a large single type of garden. I have a mix of these at our home because my land has the space for it.

When you're considering the possibilities, you can request seed catalogs from many nurseries. I have a soft spot for companies that focus on heirloom varieties and shun GMOs, but that's me. Here is a breakdown of what kinds of seeds you can find:

- **Hybrid seeds** are seeds that have been cross-pollinated to create a new seed type. This is usually done to help prevent certain diseases, or to accommodate difficult growing areas. The seeds that these plants make are not stable and cannot be saved from year to year reliably.
- **Heirloom seeds** are proven seed strains that are fifty or more years old. These plants grow and reproduce in like-kind every year, meaning you can buy once and save the seeds each year for next year's planting. My personal choice.
- **GMO seeds** are seeds that have been genetically modified using a laboratory and are usually only available to large commercial growers. These seeds are usually coated in fertilizers and have a patent on their genetic makeup, meaning if you save the seeds from your harvest you are stealing from the company that created the seeds. However, because of the genetic changes made, they can withstand pesticides and grow under many conditions. It has made large-scale food production sustainable for years. I do not agree with these practices personally, but you can decide for yourself.

Once you've looked through some of the options, it's easier to get a grasp on what your space could look like once things have grown. The catalogs either in a magazine or online can also tell you what the plant spacing needs are and what kinds of soil each plant prefers. Look for a "seed card" or "garden guide" for online purchases that gives the details.

If you want to save seeds from crops that you grow, then it's best to buy heirloom varieties that are true to seed. I usually take a few minutes each harvest to collect seeds and let them dry in a windowsill on some paper towels. I label them and keep them in an airtight container where mice can't reach them. Many seeds do need a period of time being cold in order to sprout well. To accomplish this, I use my refrigerator to cool the seeds for a few weeks to get better germination.

Helpful Gardening Terms

- **Germination** happens when a seed starts to sprout into a plant.
- **Seed soaking** is a technique used to soften the outer shell of a seed so that it's easier to sprout. It's usually done for 4–8 hours before planting.
- **Bulb forcing:** For blooms during the winter season, you can prepare your bulbs (tulips, daffodils, paperwhites, hyacinths, etc.) to bloom early by placing them in your refrigerator for a few weeks, then pulling them out and planting them in a pot in your home.
- **Seed scoring:** Some seeds need to be roughed up for their outer case to be able to sprout. This is done by scratching the seeds with a dull knife. When doing this, you are replicating a natural event in nature, like the seeds being passed through an animal's bowels, which is a common way for seeds to spread in nature.
- **Companion planting:** Some plants grow better together. This is a well-known Native American technique. You may

have read about "the three sisters" where you plant corn, beans, and squash together. This allows the corn to support the beans and lets the squash cover the ground, smothering the weeds.

- **Crop rotation:** Each year it's good to change where you plant your annual vegetables. This gives the ground the chance to rest and for different nutrients to be used and reabsorbed into the soil.
- **Pruning:** Some trees and bushes benefit from regular pruning and will produce better and bigger crops from fewer branches.
- **Cross-pollination:** Some plants cannot pollinate without another plant of the same variety nearby. Close planting of these plants is important to consider in your space.
- **Soil amendments:** Things like fire ash, eggshells, coffee grounds, and pine needles can help you change the pH of your soil over time.

To do: Take a few minutes to think about what types of gardens would fit at your home. You don't have to do them all at once, either. Maybe this year is for planting vegetables on the sunny side of your house, and next year you think about a night garden around the patio. Pray over what your family needs in this season to thrive. Maybe the bigger garden will need to wait until soccer is done, or maybe some raised garden beds will keep that soccer ball in line toward the net. Pray over these ideas and ask God to make it clear which is best for your family.

Day 2: Garden Profile

Isaiah 5 has a beautiful analogy about God planting a vineyard. God plants it in good soil, in well-tilled dirt. He plants it with wonderful grapes and keeps it safe. He does all the right things, and yet it does not give good grapes, but wild grapes instead. Isaiah then goes on to compare the vineyard to Jerusalem and the Israelite people and how it didn't matter how much God tended and cared for His people, they still rebelled and disobeyed Him. It hit home for me when I think about how much God has blessed me with, and yet I still complain. God is the best gardener and caretaker, and He outlines some key areas we need to think about: location, soil, plant choice, and caretaking.

Hopefully, you've decided on a garden type, or two, to grow in the coming years, and now we get into the details. Like, what exactly do you put into these gardens that will grow, and when? I live in West Michigan, which means we get deep winter snow and mild summers, but because I'm near Lake Michigan, I also have a strange weather pattern that the lake creates. All this information points to my unique garden zone. If you flip over a seed packet from the store, it will likely show a colorful map or list a garden zone. This tells you when in the year to plant your seeds. Since I am located so far north, there are some plants I cannot grow outdoors at all, like lemons and bananas. I can, if I utilize a greenhouse method, but those plants are off limits for me for the most part. However, if you live south of the Carolinas, you will have a hard time with plants that prefer and need cool weather to thrive, like most pine trees. So, first you need to find out your garden zone to see if you can plant what you want to plant in your garden. Ask your phone or web browser, "What is the garden zone for [add your zip code]?"

- My garden zone is: ....

The other factor is how long of a growing season you have. This is calculated as the number of days between your last frost date in the spring and your first frost date in the fall. If you're in the deep south, this may not apply to you, but it will be good to know as some plants prefer cooler temperatures while others like it hotter.

- My last frost date is: ....
- My first frost date is: ....
- My growing season is: .... days long

Next you need to think about preparing your soil. Remember last week how we talked about soil pH? Now is the time to find out what kind of soil you have and what plants you want to grow in it. You can modify the soil pH to better suit your needs. Other ways to prepare your soil includes tilling up your ground and looking for rocks if that is the garden type you've chosen. Or adding layers to your garden. Do what works best for your family. If your soil is full of clay, you may need to add some sand to make it easier to work. If your soil is gravel and sand like mine, then add loam (organic matter like leaves/compost).

- My soil type is: ....
- My pH level is: ....

In Week One, we also touched on possible garden locations around your home. Remember the compass and home map you made? Flip back to page 4 to decide which space you'd like to utilize and for what type of garden. If you've been praying and thinking about your home, then you should be starting to feel at ease about your garden location choice, garden style, and needs. The final component is caretaking. Have you allotted yourself and family enough time to take care of what you'd like to grow? If not, take time to adjust your plans to fit within your schedule, or choose something else to let go of for this season.

I have ________ hours/minutes to work on a garden each day.

Let's think about God's vineyard again in Isaiah 5. God didn't do anything wrong in how and what He planted. And yet the vineyard didn't flourish. This is where you need to let go of perfectionism. In all my years of gardening, I've successfully grown thousands of plants and I've also killed thousands of plants. Our world is fallen, it's crying out for Jesus to return. You will fail at gardening. Do not panic. You will also win at gardening. Give God the glory and keep planting.

I remember one year I was so excited to grow dahlias. They are these gorgeous blooms that can get as big as dinner plates and have more petals than you can count. So, I bought the tubers, made the soil just right, made sure we were past the frost date, planted, and waited. And waited. And waited. . . . Eventually, they came up, but by the time they were ready to bloom it was the end of August. I didn't get a single bloom before the frost killed them. I'm not going to lie, I cried.

This had been my pet project all summer and I'd failed to get even one bloom. To add to the frustration, I had to dig out all the tubers and store them all winter long to try again the next year. If I can give you one piece of advice, it would be to *be prepared to fail and have hope that you won't the next time you try.* I will say that the next year I had dozens of blooms that I enjoyed for weeks. I still don't know what I did wrong that first year and I don't know if I'll ever figure it out.

To do: Using your plant hardiness zone, make a list of plants that thrive in your area. If you don't see something you want, try searching for that particular plant with these words that may apply to you: hot/cold hardy, wet feet, arid, and pest resistant. Thank God for providing a space to garden and for a world that supports such abundant life.

Day 3: Having Enough

In Luke 12, Jesus does a deep dive into our desire to "feel like" we are provided for. Jesus takes time to point out that our feelings of discontent are often not rooted in truth. He compares our need for clothing to the flowers and how well dressed they are. He also is clear that He cares for the birds, even, who don't store up anything and yet have what they need. Yes, poverty and hunger and pain are all very real in this broken world—Jesus does not deny that. But He also says our worry should be replaced with confidence in His ability to provide, even when we can't see a way through it.

This is incredibly hard and a daily reminder for me personally. I've seen that negative bank statement; I've wondered how we would recover from physical struggles. It's real. However, I can say, looking back, that God made a way forward every single time. God's methods are often unexpected and still require work on our part, but He does provide. Take a few minutes to ask God to search your heart and help you trust Him each day to provide. God's mercies are new every morning!

Sometimes it's hard to know exactly how much to plant in the garden for your family, especially if you're trying to replace a year's worth of food in one harvest season. There are standardized lists online that will tell you exactly what to plant for the number of people in your home, but I disagree with this method and here is why: Not all families are the same. Yours is unique. Instead, go to your current pantry and look at what you actually buy and cook on a weekly basis. For example, my family loves frozen green beans, but will not touch a canned green bean even if it's coated in mushroom sauce and sprinkled with crunchy onions. By looking at your pantry, you can know what to plant. If you use marinara sauce twice a week, then you need to grow the ingredients to make it. Not sure what those are? Turn the jar around and it will tell you: tomatoes, onions, celery, and spices. If it's twice a week, then you need 104 (16-ounce) jars (52 weeks × 2) in your pantry to last all year. Start by making a list of the top ten things your family eats that you think you could grow or make instead of buying them.

Here is a list of some plants that are expensive at the store but inexpensive to grow or produce at home and have multiple uses in the kitchen. Circle the ones that interest you:

- Asparagus
- Berries
- Cabbage
- Cherries
- Cucumbers
- Garlic
- Herbs
- Honey
- Lettuces
- Maple Syrup
- Mushrooms
- Peaches
- Peppers
- Pumpkins
- Sugar Peas
- Tomatoes

Get used to looking at store items and seeing how you'd make it at home either fresh or preserving it for later. Here is a breakdown of comparing sizes of store-bought versus homemade:

Store-bought	Homemade	Weight
Tin can items, like peas	Pint jar	8 oz
Pasta sauce jar	Quart jar	16 oz
Box of mac 'n' cheese	Recipe for homemade pasta, then dried or frozen.	8 oz
Breaded chicken tenders	1 chicken portioned out, seasoned with bread coating and frozen for later.	16 oz
Jar of jelly	Half pint jar	4 oz
Bag of frozen broccoli	Blanched broccoli from the garden in quart freezer bag.	16 oz

In the years since Covid, I've seen the stores make portions smaller than in the past. In business this is called "shrinkage." So, for the same price, your mac 'n' cheese box went from 8 ounces to 6 ounces. The raspberry containers did the same. Time will tell if the big companies go back to the standard measurements of food, but for now, they seem to be enjoying the profits of shrinking the sizing, and most of us haven't noticed.

This circles back to the feeling of being provided for yet again. It's natural to worry that the stores will run out again, that the shelves will be empty when disaster hits, and that big companies will take advantage of consumers. But please don't live in fear. Yes, those things can and do happen. However, choosing to trust God is still essential even if you do have a fully stocked pantry.

This year, I've chosen not to do much canning or storing up food. Not because I have too much, but because we are expecting twins to be born

right in harvest season. When we found out, I knew I wouldn't be able to plant and tend a garden well this year. My eldest daughter realized it too; Mom wasn't going to be doing all her normal things this summer. I told her I'd just buy what we needed this year from the store like most people do. She didn't like that answer one bit, which made me smile. Then she said she would plant the garden, and I paused. I didn't want to put that burden on her. We compromised by picking out and planting her and her sister's favorite snacking plants like cherry tomatoes, sweet peas, jumbo cucumbers, and sweet peppers. Then my mom realized my dilemma and she decided to plant a bit extra in her garden to help too. God provides. It may not be what you expect and think of first, but He does. Will I can very much this year? Not at all, but we will have fresh food in season, and I am thankful for that.

To do: Make a list of foods your family buys every week and decide if growing them would be a better choice for your family. Pray over larger plants that live long term, like fruit trees and other perennial plants. Using a piece of graph paper, begin to lay out how much room you have to plant and if you will need to supplement with a trip to the farmers market or by trading with a fellow gardening friend. Read Luke 12 and ask God to provide in the coming year.

Day 4: Plant Types

Did you know that Jesus enjoyed flowers? In Matthew 6:28–29 it says, “So why do you worry about clothing? Consider the lilies of the field, how they grow: they neither toil nor spin; and yet I say to you that even Solomon in all his glory was not arrayed like one of these.” In Israel, where Jesus was teaching, the lilies that grow are our classic Easter lily. I find this amazing, that Jesus considers something made by God in its natural form so stunning compared to what the culture said was glorious. God’s beauty in creation is timeless. Don’t be afraid to plant for the beauty of the plant as this gives a harvest of joy that is just as valid and wonderful as a jar of canned peaches.

God has created so many plant types to consider for a garden and landscape. Think about what your family would use and, if space is limited, which plants you could trade or barter with a friend. One of the main considerations for long-term planting is whether a plant survives for one season or for longer. When a plant dies and does not come back, it’s considered an annual plant. Most garden vegetables are considered annual, like tomatoes, pumpkins, and cucumbers. In my northern area, peppers can’t make it through a winter, making them an annual plant; however, in southern areas, many pepper plants will live for more than one season with proper care.

When a plant has a two-year cycle, it’s called a biennial plant. Many root vegetables are biennials, like carrots, onions, and garlic. An example of a biennial fruit would be raspberries and blackberry brambles. When a plant lives for more than three years, it’s considered a perennial plant. This includes trees, shrubs (like blueberries), asparagus, herbs, and rhubarb. Think carefully about where you plant a perennial plant as it can be hard to move them later without damaging them.

Trees: Tree perennials take a long time to grow and produce. Think about the final size of the tree and if pruning will be necessary to keep it in check and healthy.

Shrubs: Shrubs are perennials in most areas. A shrub can range in size from 2 feet to around 12 feet in circumference. Be sure enough space is available around them to get the best harvests and for picking.

Vines can be perennial like grapes, or annual like cucumbers and watermelons.

Brambles are biennial, growing the canes in year one and producing fruit in year two. Year three canes will need to be pruned and removed. Brambles often have thorns.

Flowers can be perennials like roses, peonies and hostas. Or biennial like foxgloves and hollyhocks. Or annuals like petunias and impatiens.

Vegetables: Most often annual and rotational planting is encouraged for vegetables, as different plants use the soil in different ways. Some are perennials like asparagus, rhubarb, and peppers (if you live in the South). Some biennial plants include carrots, beets, cabbage, and kale.

Fruits: Many fruits come from trees, but garden fruits include melons and tomatoes, which are annual plants.

Microgreens and sprouts: These are super short-lived and are picked before reaching maturity, usually within a month or less. They are easy to grow indoors and are delicious.

Herbs: A mix of annual, biennial, and perennial, depending on your garden zone.

Like I said earlier, my garden ended up being planted on the corner of our front yard where all the neighbors can see. In order to make it appealing, I decided to create a structure with my perennial plants. So, for the two side edges of the garden, I have one row of thornless blackberries, and on the mirror side, I have heirloom raspberries, both on a matching trellis system. This gives me a nice planting space between the two rows for my annual vegetables and herbs.

I also created a focal point in the garden by putting up a third trellis for grapes and hanging a wind chime in honor of a passed loved one. Essentially, I've created a garden room that I can fill with plants and switch around. It also means, if things don't get weeded, it's a bit hard to tell because of the edges being sided with berry bushes. This layout would not work if you wanted to use a tractor to till things up, because there isn't the space to make a pass through. Think about what kind of equipment you want to use and that will help direct you with what to plant and where to plant it.

There are a few ways to get plants for your homestead. The easiest thing to do is walk into your local plant nursery and see what they have. Most everything will be good for your area and the staff should be able to help you with any questions you have. You should be able to buy the following types of plants:

- **Starts:** Plants that have already been started on their growing journey and will take less time to produce. A great choice if you're new to gardening or if you are late getting things planted.
- **Seed packets:** My favorite way to grow things as it's cost effective and fun to watch as they grow. However, it takes space, time, and lighting to keep the seedlings alive until planting time.
- **Pots:** These are usually larger plants that grow year after year. These are your structural plants that can create a garden room feel when planted strategically.
- **Bare root:** Plants that look nearly dead but are far from it. These are usually small trees or asparagus starts that need to be planted immediately for best results. If I want to buy these, I will often dig and prepare my space first and then purchase so I can immediately plant them. Check with your local conservation district office for native plant varieties.

- **Bulbs and tubers:** Common with some flowers like dahlias, tulips, iris, peonies, and potatoes, these plants look like round or thick roots and will come up once planted correctly.

Use the grid on the opposite page to draw out some layout ideas for your garden space. You can find lots of plans online too, but it's important to consider what you have already if you want your garden design to flow well with the rest of your home and garden. For example, if you have a small garden space near the back door of your home, that may be a great spot for herbs and other plants you'd like to pick quickly while you're cooking dinner. But you may want to have bigger crops in a dedicated space a bit farther away. It's entirely up to you!

A quick note about watering your garden. It's important to place your garden where you can get a water hose to if need be. Other options include a pump system from a pond or river, or rain barrel collections. You can water your plants in a few ways:

- **Overhead watering** is when you use a hose or sprinkler system to mimic rain and drench the whole plant. This works best in the early morning or late evening when the chance of evaporation is lessened. However, some plants tend to get mildew issues if they retain the moisture on their leaves for too long.
- **Ground watering:** Using soaker hoses and mulching. This can be an effective way to save water over time and limit the amount of evaporation. However, the cost of these hoses and systems can be a bit higher than a traditional sprinkler system.
- **Hand watering:** This is when you fill a watering can and water plants individually. It takes much longer but is also nostalgic and fun to do. You also have much more control over how each individual plant is watered, whether from overhead or at the ground level. This also lets you focus on and inspect everything you water.

Here is a quick breakdown of common vegetable (and one herb) types:

- **Tomatoes** have three common sizes: Beefsteak (large, round, and juicy), Roma (medium, oblong, and meaty), and cherry (small and sweet).
- **Beans** can grow either on a vine or as a small bush.
- **Cucumbers** can either be for pickling or for eating fresh.
- **Bell peppers** come in many colors, but green is how they all start out.
- **Corn** can be decorative, for livestock, or sweet, for people.
- **Basil** has several types: purple, Thai, lemon, and sweet.

To start planting seeds in your garden, you will need a few extra things. The first is seed starting soil (fluffy and holds water well). Next, a container, which can be as simple as a stack of dixie cups or as advanced as specialized trays from the store. You'll need good water that has no additives like salt or fluoride, etc. A light source is essential, whether you use a sunny window or if you snag some grow lights online. Lastly, seeds will not sprout if they think it's cold, so you'll need a heating mat or to make sure your growing space is above 60°F.

To do: Take a few moments to review what types of plants you already have around your home. Are they annuals, biennials, or perennials? Are they in a location you'd like them to stay long term, or will they need to be moved around? Take a prayer walk around your yard and ask God to guide you as you seek to build a garden that serves Him and your family well.

Day 5: Weeds

Every gardener's nemesis is weeds. So. Many. Weeds. Not only do they multiply without effort, but they are hard to remove, too. There are so many options for weed treatments including:

- **Suppression:** Things like mulch, tarps, cardboard, or garden fabric are all ways to keep the weeds flattened down but can be expensive and hard to maintain.
- **Pulling:** Digging them out by hand or with tools is a great way to ensure you get all the roots and prevent them from returning. As a kid, my mom would pay fifty cents for every five-gallon bucket of weeds we filled, and we valued the work.

- **Chemicals:** The only time I will use chemicals for killing plants at my home is in the case of poison ivy (which I am terribly allergic to). You can use herbicides to kill garden weeds, and many people do, but after doing research I believe that the long-term cost of soil contamination is not worth it for our family.
- **Boiling water:** If you really want to pour something on the weeds and forget them, then I recommend filling your tea kettle with boiling water and pouring it on each weed individually, being careful not to touch plants you want to keep. This will scald the weed and kill it. This is only sustainable for small areas, usually, like sidewalk cracks and troublesome spots.
- **Goats:** If you need a large area cleaned up, then renting a few goats can be a fast and effective way to clear an area. An added bonus is that goats will even eat poison ivy without any repercussions to themselves or you.

- **Ground cover:** Picking a plant like clover, sunflowers, or barley to grow as a ground cover is a way to amend your soil naturally and keep the weeds down.

All of these methods have pros and cons, but what if most weeds aren't as bad as we think they are? At my house we do not have the beautiful, curated lawn, but a patchwork of "weeds" mixed with grass. I love it. My kids pick bouquets of dandelions for my kitchen. White clover feeds the bees. I've even found edible morel mushrooms popping up between mowings. The weeds are often far more helpful than you realize if you just take a few minutes to learn about them.

As I write this, I confess I've often considered some people in my life like weeds—annoying, in the way, taking up space, and not worth my time. But God says otherwise. 1 Peter 2:17a says, "Honor all people." That's a big thing to ask when I feel like a person is on my last nerve. The Strongs Concordance defines the word "honor" in this verse as, "to revere or to find value." God calls us to find the value in every person, even when it's hard. You don't have to choose to be around them, but to see their value as a person made in the image of God. As we learn about weeds and begin to see their value, we don't have to use them, but we should recognize they do have value as a part of God's amazing creation. Pray with me to see that even the frustrating people in your life have value as God's image bearers.

Here are some weeds that have amazing benefits and may be something you want to look for in your area:

- **Dandelion:** Good for bees, edible flowers, leaves, and roots.
- **Purslane:** Edible leaves, high in vitamins, ground cover.
- **Broadleaf plantain:** Medicinal for stings and bites.
- **Mullein:** Medicinal for respiratory issues, attracts pollinators, biennial.
- **Chicory:** Medicinal for digestion, roots make a decaf coffee substitute, beautiful blooms.
- **Clover:** Fixes nitrogen in soil, prevents erosion, edible flowers, great for bees.

Genesis 1:31a says, "Then God saw everything that He had made, and indeed it was very good." Not just some things or most things, but everything. Yes, this is before the fall of Adam and Eve, but sin doesn't erase all the good that God made. It complicates it and stains it, but we can still do what Peter says and look to honor people and the world around us by finding the value.

To do: Think of one person who you have given "weed" status to and ask God to change your heart and mind about that person. Pray before you encounter this person that God gives you eyes to see the value in him or her. Choose one of the weeds either listed above or in your area and research it to find the value that God created it to have.

Grow

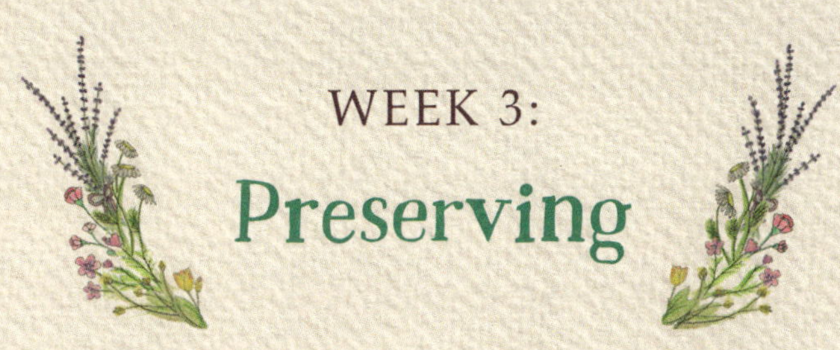

WEEK 3:

Preserving

Now that you've dedicated your home, have decided where to start, and planned a garden, it's time to look at preserving all the things that you will grow. In Psalm 107:37, God's loving-kindness and goodness is extended in part through fruitful harvest for those who call on Him. This week will be a time to learn how to preserve the harvests that God gives us with the intent to bless not only our families but those around us as well.

In Bible times, in the book of Genesis, there was a great famine that extended from Egypt all through Israel and beyond. But God had a plan. God had put Joseph through a lot of struggles where he learned how to first manage a flock of sheep for his father, then a whole household for Potiphar, and then an entire jail for Pharaoh, until God placed him as second in command of the entire nation of Egypt. Joseph got busy and for seven bountiful years he faithfully stored up grain. God did this to protect not only His chosen people but many people from a seven-year famine.

As we learn the different ways to store up food this week, remember to be like Joseph and be generous with what you store up, because it was God's bountiful harvest first that He has entrusted you to manage well for His kingdom works. Pray that God gives you a sharing heart as you store up your harvest and to remove fears that creep in to spoil the blessing that God has provided.

Day 1: Canning Foods

When people think of homesteading, one of the top things that comes to mind is canning. Canning is the process of heating glass jars full of produce so that they seal and can be stored for years on a shelf. I grew up canning, and it's one of my go-to ways to preserve food. However, it can feel incredibly intimidating because things can go wrong quickly.

Proverbs 30:24–25 has an interesting saying: "There are four things which are little on the earth, but they are exceedingly wise: The ants are a people not strong, yet they prepare their food in the summer . . ." Ants are of little consequence by the world's standards—not strong, fairly common to find—and yet God calls ants wise for how they store up their food for later. If homesteading has made you feel like you're not living up to other's standards, or if it's displaying your weaknesses because you have to rely on God, or if it sometimes feels pointless because you can get a jar of pickles at the grocery store anytime, then you may feel like an ant, just like I do. And maybe that's exactly the point God's trying to make. God's view of His creation is unique and true. So, if God says an ant is wise because he stores up food for later, then we are in good company.

Canning falls into a couple of categories and some recipes are easier than others. I'm going to break them down here for you to see.

Type	Difficulty Level	Foods	Equipment Needs
Pressure canning	Harder due to learning curve of equipment and capacity for things to go wrong.	Anything a water bath can do plus meats, dairy, any low acid vegetables.	Pressure canner, jar tongs, funnel, canning jars, lids, and rings
Water bath or steam canning	Fairly simple as long as times and safety rules are followed.	Pickled foods, jams, tomato foods, fruits. Anything with either high acid or high sugar.	Large pot that can cover jars with water, jar tongs, funnel, canning jars, lids, and rings

What I'm hoping you can see with this table is that you can do some canning without a pressure canner and it's very safe, as long as you follow the directions. However, if you want the option to can meats, dairy, and low acid vegetables, then pressure canning is for you.

There is basic science behind why canning works, and it's not as obscure as you may think. In fourth grade science, we learned that when something is heated up, it causes molecules to bounce around more, creating heat and therefore expanding slightly. When things are cooled down, the molecules slow down and become more stable, making them smaller. When you do these actions quickly by water bath canning or pressure canning a jar of food, you heat it up, making things expand, then take them out and let them cool, so they get smaller. This forces the rubber seal on the canning rings to create a vacuum effect, and *pop*! Your jar seals do not allow any air or contaminants into your jar. It's fun food science and to do it well there are a few potholes to watch out for:

- **Timing:** It's important to heat up each jar according to its size so that it gets hot all the way to the center of the jar.
- **Filling:** When you fill a jar, it helps to start with foods that are already hot. You will see recipes that call for hot pack or cold pack. Hot packing is the safest method as it stops the glass jars from having shock (and breaking) when you place them into the canner.
- **Cleanliness:** Having jars that are clean and sterile (easy to do in the dishwasher) is important so that your food stays fresh a long time. Cleaning the tops of the jars before setting the lids and rings on is important as well so that jars don't siphon out the tops or break the seals later.
- **Head space:** Keeping some air at the top of the jar is essential so that the vacuum seal (*pop!*) can happen as the jars cool down.

- **Sugars and acids:** Using sugar and acid is a natural way to preserve food. Bacteria can't handle it, and therefore it makes these items more shelf stable so they don't need to be heated as high as they would be in the pressure canner. Don't skimp on less sugar or low acid vinegar as it's not worth the risk of losing all your food and time working on this.
- **Recipes:** Most recipes from reputable sources are tested and tried well. Don't modify them unless you are certain that your food will stay fresh in the jars.
- **Contamination:** Don't can something that is already going bad. Cut out the areas affected by mold or that are past prime. If you don't, you will risk contaminating the whole jar, or worse, the whole batch of food.

I had an instance once where we were canning applesauce with our elderly neighbors. They had some health concerns and requested no sugar be added to the apples. I agreed. I also regretted it a couple of months later when I started opening the jars and seeing splotches of mold at the top of each jar. I ended up throwing away so much applesauce and wasting a whole day's worth of work in the kitchen. If I had taken the time to pressure can the applesauce, then adding no sugar would not have been an issue. However, because we water bath canned them instead, the seal wasn't strong enough and the sugar wasn't there to protect the food from molding. Don't be like me. Understand the process, follow the recipe, and keep your kitchen clean.

To do: One of the major considerations with canning is where you are going to store the food once it's canned in your jars. We have space in our basement on some sturdy shelving. Think about and select a space for your canned items. We call our little basement room a harvest room and keep other stored foods there too, including our deep freezer. Once you have chosen a space, then think about what you may need to get to make it perform well, like shelving, a dehumidifier, or a bit of extra lighting. Take a few minutes to pray over the space that will be your storeroom or cupboard. Invite God to bless your work and to keep your focus on His provision rather than self-sufficiency.

Day 2: Fermenting Foods

Fermenting has taken on a whole new identity in the last few years, making it one of the trendiest things you can try. There's a good chance you've dabbled in sourdough, cheese, sauerkraut, kimchi, beer/wine, kombucha, or fizzy sodas in the last year with some success and probably some failure as well. Fermentation can create some amazing food for eating and for our health. Here is a list of some of the pros and cons of each of these fermentations:

Fermentation	Difficulty	Equipment Needs	Monetization Possibilities
Sourdough breads	Medium	Low	Very good
Beers/wines	Low to Medium	Medium	State regulated
Cheese	Medium to High	High	Often state regulated
Sauerkraut	Low	Low	Low
Kimchi	Medium	Low	Medium
Fizzy Sodas	Medium	Medium	Often state regulated

Fermenting has a long history and was one of the best ways to preserve food prior to refrigeration. If you're like me, you've had a few fermentation experiments that end up bubbling over and in one case even exploding. It happens. In Luke 5:37–39, Jesus speaks a short parable about putting new wine into old wine skins, and what happens? The skin bags burst and spill the wine, ruining it. Now Jesus is not really teaching about the best ways to make food or wine; what he's really after here is that sometimes the old method simply won't work when you put a new thing into it.

Jesus is talking about the old law of Moses and how it was a temporary placeholder until He could come and make all things new and bring His new covenant of forgiveness through His own sacrifice. But He is met with resistance in verse 39 as the Israelites want to keep the old ways instead of seeing the newness through Him. In our culture, we are often told the lie that we can "have it all" or "you can do it all." But just like the Israelites would have to move on from the old law of Moses to step into redemption through Christ, we must also step out of some of our old ways of doing things to embrace what God wants for us going forward. Just like an old cheese or wine, the effects of gradual change over time have big and amazing results. Take a few moments to pray and ask God to show you areas in your life where you are holding on to old ways that no longer fit with what He wants for you now.

Regardless of what you are fermenting, there are a few ways to tell if things are working the right way:

- If you are using a brine, look for the brine to be cloudy, not clear.
- Keep an eye on the level of the liquid in the jar; it should be staying above the vegetables. You may need to weigh it down to get this.
- Look for bubbles coming to the top of your ferment.
- Color changes should be happening, going from bright and fresh to duller. Don't compare the color of your pickles to store-bought ones because they often add coloring agents to commercial jars for appearances.

I love making a quick ferment in the summer when produce is everywhere. The fun part of this quick fermenting is that you can totally customize it to your needs as long as you know the ratios. I use quart jars because they are easy to work with and a good size for my family, but you can size this up or down as long as you keep the same ratios. Another thing to keep in mind with any fermentation is that it needs to be able to let air out of the jar as the natural fermentation process has a gas byproduct. You can be as simple, like a tea towel over top with a rubber band, or as fancy as a weighted glass puck, or as unique as a smooth rock you foraged from your local beach.

Quick Lactofermented Veggie Medley Recipe

1. In a quart mason jar, add all your veggies, such as cucumber slices, frenched carrots, onion slivers, and turnip wedges. You don't have to have a medley of veggies; if you want to stick with classic cucumbers, that's fine too.
2. Add 1 clove of garlic (or 2 if you love it like we do). You can also add other spices like dill, basil, clove, bay leaf, or hot pepper. Be creative with your flavors!
3. Add 2 tablespoons of salt. If you are using a pint size jar, then do ½ tablespoon. If you're using a larger jar, then size it up. The ratio you want is 1:2, meaning for every 1 cup of water you need to add 1 tablespoon of salt.
4. Add water to the top, making sure your veggies stay below the water line. If they are above it then they will rot. You can add a cabbage leaf to keep things from floating, or a glass fermentation weight, or even a very clean smooth rock (I find these on our local Great Lake Beaches). Add the lid and shake it well, making sure the salt dissolves. If you have a fermentation lid, then great. Otherwise, putting a towel or napkin over top with a rubber band will work too. The goal

is to let air escape the jar so that it won't explode as things ferment. Place the jar in a spot not to be moved for 3–10 days. As it ferments, you can check the taste. Move it to the fridge once you are happy with it.

I remember one Christmas we were all helping in the kitchen, getting meals prepped and ready for family arrival. The excitement was coursing through me. I asked my mom (again), "What can I help with next?"

"We need to make room in the fridge for the veggie tray; can you clean out some things?"

I nodded and set to my task of finding expired foods and tossing them, rearranging, and wiping down the shelves. My fingers landed on a jar in the back that was oozing all over the shelf. It smelled, so I decided it had to go. Later that day my mom went to make the rolls (everyone's favorite part of dinner), but she couldn't find her ingredients in the clean fridge. She described the jar, and my face went whiter than the snowbanks outside. I'd unwittingly thrown away her sourdough starter batch that she was going to use to make rolls. I felt horrible. My siblings said I'd "ruined Christmas dinner," and I'd have to say they were right. We all missed out on dinner rolls that year. But I wouldn't ever make that mistake again. What looked like a mess to me was actually working perfectly, and I just lacked the knowledge to know it at the time.

To do: Think about if fermentation is right for you and your family. For health reasons or for enjoyment, fermenting is an amazing example of how God has created food to change over time. Choose one of these fermentations to add to your routine and see how it goes. Pray over it as you seek God's will in all areas of your home and life.

Day 3: Dehydrating & Smoking Foods

Dehydrating foods goes back so far in time that nearly every culture uses it in some way. Most historians agree that dried food was the first form of preservation used. Whether it's spices, fish, or fruits, people have been using the wind and sun to dehydrate since the beginning. In James 4, the Bible talks about our lives being like "a vapor that appears for a little time and then vanishes away." This reference would have been easily understood in biblical times as many families would dry dates and grapes on rooftops, and fish would be laid out near the seaside to dry before taking them into the market. These methods are still used today in many places.

In my kitchen, I usually resort to a dehydrator or my oven to speed up the drying process. My high humidity Michigan climate isn't suited for air drying very often. One other problem I have found with drying is long-term storage. Humidity tends to find its way into my jars and cause mold. So, I invested in a vacuum sealer for mason jars (about $25 online). It sucks the air out of the jar, creating a seal without the need to add oxygen packets or other preservatives. Some people will use salt or rice to help absorb moisture in dried foods, too.

When Jesus feeds the five thousand in Matthew 14, He starts with five loaves and two fish. The fish in this instance would almost certainly have been dried so that it could last longer than the three days the crowd had already been in the desert listening to Jesus.

For dried foods to have great shelf life, I've found using glass canning jars and a jar vacuum sealer has the best results. The glass keeps things from being contaminated and the vacuum seal keeps out moisture. You can also use oxygen absorbing packets if you prefer. A third option is a freeze dryer. These high-tech investments come with a big price tag but allow you to preserve literally anything. Here is a list of foods that are easily dried and stored for later use using a regular dehydrator or the lowest setting in your oven:

- Beans
- Carrots
- Fish
- Fruit rolls
- Garlic
- Herbs
- Mushrooms
- Pasta
- Peas
- Pumpkins
- Spices
- Teas

One of our favorite things to dry these past few years is catnip. Not only does it have wonderful medical uses for people, but our cat loves it. I make packets of it to give as gifts and to sell as well. Other things you can make with dried items include soaps, herb blends, tea bags, pressed flowers, and edible flower sprinkles.

Smoking is another great way to dehydrate food and add amazing flavor to it. If you don't have a smoker, you can improvise using a grill or open fire. Some foods that are common to smoke include: fish, meat, squash, sausages, cheeses, nuts, berries, and hard-boiled eggs. Using smoke to cure foods is a preservation technique that requires hardwood as the burning agent. Using pine wood is not recommended due to the pitch inside the wood.

To do: Make a list of the foods you currently use or purchase that are dried. Decide which of those items you think you can make at home instead of buying at the store. Starting simple is good and trying a few different options when you have extra produce is a good idea. Pray over your pantry space and ask God to help you be humble as you remember that each of our lives is like a vapor and is short. Ask God to give you insight on the best way to use your time while you have it.

Day 4: Freezing Foods

Most Americans, myself included, don't even consider that refrigeration is a luxury for most of the world. I toss things into the freezer all the time thinking, "I'll get to that later." Sometimes I do and sometimes that bag of frozen tomatoes is still there two summers later. Honestly, most things do freeze extremely well, even with minimal prep work. The trick is understanding expansion.

Living in the cold north of Michigan winters, I've seen this over and over. Once when I was young, I wanted to make an igloo and realized my plastic mold I had carefully filled inside and brought outside to freeze did freeze, but also shattered the plastic into hunks. Then again as a teen, I put my Coke outside in a snowbank to get a quick cool down and forgot it was there. The metal can exploded, sending slushy coke across the yard. Then, as an adult, I thought I was supposed to be calm and controlled and not need anyone—solid, like a block of ice. Until one day my emotions exploded out of me, leaving a trail of hurt feelings. I hadn't been praying or taking my worries to God. The reality check was hard, and God slowly put me back together. He taught me that, like a glass or hard plastic container in the freezer, I'll explode if I try to hold too much inside!

In 2 Peter 1:5–8 there is a beautiful list of things that increase over time as you walk in the faith, like virtue, knowledge, perseverance, goodliness, kindness, and love. It's a similar list to the fruits of the Spirit, but what I love is the description that they should continue to grow as you mature. What an amazing example of expansion that will cause abounding joy and peace for each of us.

Whatever food you put into your freezer will expand, and whether you are using plastic bags, Tupperware, or mason jars, you will need to accommodate the expansion. In my effort to reduce waste, I've been using wide-mouth mason jars, the same ones that I use to can with for my freezer foods and have had great success as long as I don't overfill them. Here are some ideas for freezer foods to get you started:

- ¼ or ½ a cow bought from a local farmer
- Smoothy kits with frozen berries, kale, or juice cubes
- Premade crockpot or lasagna meals ready to heat up
- Shredded zucchini or apples for quick bread

There are some who prefer to blanch foods before they freeze them. Blanching is the process of dunking fresh produce (usually vegetables) into boiling water and then into ice water. The goal with blanching is to first kill any bacteria and second to stop the produce from turning to mush when it's thawed out. I personally don't blanch, and I have good reason for it for my family. I freeze vegetables that need to be cooked to be eaten, like peas, corn, carrots,

and broccoli. So, when I go to eat the frozen vegetables, I put them directly into a pot of boiling water while they are still frozen. This is essentially blanching but in backwards order. It saves me time in summer when the harvest is in full swing and speeds up my cooking later. This is an example of something I'm doing that works for my family, but not all families will choose this route and that's totally fine. What I'm hoping is that you understand the process so you can make an informed decision for what would be best for your family.

In order to keep food from getting lost in the deep freezer, I use a twelve-month method. I take twelve reusable shopping bags and divide my freezer food between each bag. So if I have twelve packages of frozen peas, I put one in each month's bag. If I get freezer beef, I divide out the meat between the twelve bags, six pounds of burger, three steaks, etc. Then at the beginning of each month I move one freezer bag to my upstairs kitchen freezer as the month's foods to eat and add them to my meal prep list. This stops waste due to freezer burn and makes sure food stays fresh and not lost at the bottom.

To do: Consider starting the twelve-month system in your freezer. Pray over 2 Peter 1:5–8, that God will continue to multiply His presence in your heart and life. Ask the Holy Spirit to grow and nurture your faith in each area.

Day 5: Cold Storing Foods

When I think of cold storage, my mind goes to little hobbit holes dug into the side of a hillside—impractical but romantic. In reality, my cold storage is a small chilly room in my basement. It can also be a spot in the garage or anywhere that is protected from freezing temperatures but still stays below 50 degrees or so. It's wherever works best for you. If you live in a warmer

environment, then underground may be the only place you can find to keep things cool.

There are many things that store well in cooler temps that don't need to be refrigerated. Our little basement room is called the "harvest room" because I keep most things in it like:

- Apples
- Canned goods
- Carrots
- Dried foods
- Flour
- Flower bulbs
- Potatoes
- Soap
- Squash
- Sugar
- Yams

When it comes to keeping things stored up, the Bible is clear in Matthew 6:19–21. We should not be trying to lay up treasure here on Earth, but treasure in heaven. Here on Earth, things go bad, even with our best efforts. This fall I had a major issue with mice in my harvest room—so gross. Not only did I end up throwing out damaged food, but also sanitizing a room that is not easily cleaned. Moving full canning jars shelf by shelf to vacuum and then spray with cleaner was not a fun endeavor. Thankfully, our future with Jesus has no such issues. No rust or mold. No thieves to steal.

I confess that this hits hard for me. For years I worked catching shoplifters, and then after that, at an insurance company who paid out over and over again for break-ins and damages. It's so common even in the "country" where I live. It's inescapable. And yet God says, "do not worry," both before and after this storage tip in Matthew 6. I don't think that was a mistake to bookend our treasures with warnings about worry. Take a few minutes to pray over your cold storage room. Ask God to fill your heart with peace that passes understanding. Even if it all goes away, it will still be okay, because God is in control.

If your heart is still set on the romantic hobbit hole cold storage from earlier, I don't blame you. There are several methods for making cold storage that not only keep the temperature low but also the pests out. Consider lining walls with cinderblock or fieldstone and cementing between them. Another method is to use haybales and clay to create an insulated storage in the ground. Or, if you're in a recycling mood, I have a friend who took her broken chest freezer and buried it up to its lid to store potatoes, carrots, and apples.

To do: It's time to start making a journal of what you have stored up here on Earth. Not so much as a way to "be prepared," but instead to show to yourself the provision of God year after year. If you are unsure where to start, you can get a copy of my *Homestead Journal* on Amazon.

FOUR

WEEK 4: Cooking

Cooking is one of my favorite things to do. Whether it's an old recipe I know by heart or I'm trying something new, cooking fills me with hope, joy, and remembering. God has made food and sharing a table at the heart of His gospel message. With its roots deep in the Passover meal, we celebrate the Lord's Supper as the new covenant brought by Jesus. The Eucharist brings joy though Jesus's salvation, hope for a tomorrow growing in the Holy Spirit's sanctification, and remembrance for all that God has already done through time.

Just like Jesus calls us to His table to remember His sacrifice for our sins, cooking calls us to remember, too. We remember people who crafted the recipes we love most. We remember the past seasons and the work that went into getting those preserved items stored away. We remember to then teach the next generation how to do the same. Teaching my kids how to cook well is high on my priority list for a few reasons. I want them to know where food comes from and the time it takes to make it. I want them to have the health benefits of making things at home versus buying premade foods. I want them to enjoy the simplicity of eating meals together and having that connection that seems to have gone missing in our world so often.

As we move through this week, we will talk about lots of ways to cook and use what we have preserved. Moreso, we will talk about the hospitality that comes with sharing a table together with others who are both like us and also different. Just like Jesus ate with all types of people, we should do the same with the goal of spreading the hope, joy, and remembrance to those we invite to our table. Take a few moments to listen to the song, "Come to the Table" by Sidewalk Prophets and pray that God makes your home a place of hospitality for those who need Him.

Day 1: Scratch vs. Almost Scratch vs. Store-bought

When I first started this homestead journey, I thought I had to make everything at home as purely as possible. It took me a few years to understand that there is a balance between what you have time to do and what you want to do. This section is all about figuring out that balance for your family.

If you're looking into the homestead lifestyle, then I'm sure you've noticed the pedestal that "made from scratch" foods are put on. But you do not have to make things homemade all the time. In fact, if you try, you will run out of time. For example, for sourdough to really be made from scratch, you will also have to mill your own flour, which is totally possible and great but not easy. Hence my category of "almost made from scratch," because I buy flour and sugar and other ingredients to create my meals and snacks. Here is the ratio I have at my house, and you can decide what yours is:

- 25% made from scratch: meaning the ingredients are grown, preserved, and milled at my home where I control all the ingredient details. This is super localized food that is highly nutritious and takes the most time to preserve and then cook with.

- 60% are almost made from scratch: meaning I buy basic ingredients to then create our food and snacks, like canned beans, flour, and sugar. This is a sweet spot for us because I can control most of the factors I need to make our food healthy without spending all my time in the kitchen.
- 15% store-bought: meaning I bought something totally premade that can be eaten right out of the package like mac 'n' cheese, roasted chicken, or a freezer meal. Even in this category I'm looking for organic options as often as I can.

Your family's ratios may be different than mine, and these numbers change as the season of life dictates. For example, I am currently pregnant with twins due in late July, at peak harvest season. So, I have chosen to do less gardening and preserving than I have in the past because it's too hard right now. That's totally okay! You have to take each season in stride. What about your family? What would your ratios be? What do you wish they were?

- ____% Made from scratch but I want it to be ____%
- ____% Almost made from scratch but my goal is ____%
- ____% Store-bought but I wish it was ____%

In Genesis 27, we read about another made-from-scratch meal, and its stakes are high—a birthright is in play, but first a meal must be made. Isaac wanted to bless his first-born son Esau before he dies and asks him to hunt wild game and make him his favorite savory dish. Esau agrees and goes out hunting. Meanwhile, Jacob and his mother Rebekah decide to make the meal at home using two young goats from the flock. Once the food is ready, Jacob disguises himself as his older brother and obtains the birthright from his father, leaving Esau with nothing. This lie breaks the family apart for years.

It's important that we don't obsess over how much food we make from scratch. Is all food equal? No. But food made from the right heart place brings blessings, not curses. So instead of bursting with pride over whether you hunted down the steak yourself or praising the great deal you got at your local butcher, remember the heart of the food is hospitality. It's about bringing people together in peace for blessings and not for conflict and curses. Pray over your heart and ask God to remove the prejudice around food that can often cause offense.

Let's take a quick moment to talk about allergies here. Whether it's gluten or dairy or dyes, there are many things contributing to digestion troubles for everyone in America. A lot of it has to do with the overuse of super-processed foods, seed oils, and lack of nutrition education. There are whole books written about this and it's good to investigate and be aware of. But again, keep your heart in check as you visit a friend's home, and they serve you a meal that is less than made from scratch. Not everyone has the time or means to prepare a meal the same way you might. I also won't turn down a drive-through meal if that's what my family needs at that moment. You don't have to be a 100 percent on anything other than your love for Jesus.

Another area to consider is the health impact of the pans, utensils, and service ware you use in your kitchen. We avoid plastic as it tends to degrade over time, contaminating foods. I also don't use any form of "nonstick" cookware because again the coatings wear off and get into the food you're cooking. That being said, making the switch in this category is super expensive. To get around the price tag of cast iron and stainless steel, I seek out secondhand items. Some of the best places to look at are:

- **Secondhand shops:** Places like Goodwill and Salvation Army will have kitchen odds and ends from time to time.
- **Estate sales:** These are a great way to find a matching set of dinnerware, pots and pans, or expensive knives for a super reduced price.
- **Yard sales:** Sometimes you will stumble onto a treasure that the current owner has taken for granted.

After a good cleaning, secondhand items often have lots of life left to them. I also don't mind the curated look of mismatched things as long as they serve a good purpose in my kitchen. Look for brand names that are known for quality when you're out thrifting so you know you're getting the best deal you can.

To do: Make a meal plan for each category of food your family uses. For example, we have extra things to do on Wednesdays, and those days I often serve premade or purchased meals. But on slow days, we use the mostly from-scratch option and use up our canned goods and frozen foods. Pray for what works best for your family and the time you have available. Pray that God clears your heart of judgment when it comes to eating out or eating at another family's home.

Day 2: Offsetting Costs & Quality of Life

I'm going to be 100 percent honest and say that the homestead lifestyle is typically not cheaper. The time, equipment, and products will cost more to grow and make yourself, especially at first. So, why bother? The answer is quality of life. To know where and how your food was grown, or how clean your water is, or how toxin-free your cleaning has become does give a type of peace. But it will never be a stand-in for God's peace.

In 1 Corinthians 6:19–20, it talks about how much God cares how we treat our bodies. It says: "Or do you not know that your body is the temple of the Holy Spirit who is in you, whom you have from God, and you are not your own? For you were bought at a price; therefore, glorify God in your body and in your spirit, which are God's." Did you catch it? Part of the trinity of God *lives* inside us! If that isn't a good enough reason to take care of ourselves, then let's finish the verse, because the "price" that you were bought with is the blood of Jesus. That is a double reason to take great care about how we live our lives. Pray that God lets the weight of those verses sink in. Not in a superficial "be fit and healthy" sort of way, but in a "I am a walking temple of God" way that shakes us to our core.

If you're looking for affordable ways to stock your home with clean ingredients and good kitchen tools for the quality of life you long for, these are some of the best methods I've found:

- **Bulk Buying:** I have a family of eight, so this is a favorite method of mine, but even a small family can buy in bulk or share a bulk buy with a friend. The goal of buying large quantities is to save on packaging costs and middle sellers. Be careful not to buy more than you can use up before it expires; otherwise, you've wasted your investment. Look into the best way to store your bulk items to get the best lifespan you can from them.
- **Bartering:** Do you have access to produce in large quantities? We have a big field of elderberries and access to beef fat that I render into tallow products. These two things allow me to trade for a lot of items that I don't produce myself, like maple syrup and honey. Look at what God has blessed you with and see if you can use it as a trading opportunity with others.
- **Seconds:** This is a farming word for produce that is two or more days old or close to going bad and is therefore discounted greatly. The best way to get these deals is to visit farm markets near closing time and ask if they have any deals on seconds. No farmer wants to take home that extra produce if they can help it, and they will often reduce the price to get it off their hands.
- **Secondhand:** I love a good thrift store and finding the right piece of canning equipment on a dusty shelf still makes me smile. There are plenty of online secondhand places that you can check for cost savings as well. Don't assume you have to buy it new or that new is better; I've

often opted for the dented stainless pans at the thrift store rather than the new nonstick toxic options at the department store.

The next area of savings I've found is cleaning products. Not only are most cleaning products at the store expensive, but they are also highly toxic to our bodies. When I first married my husband, I discovered he had sensitive skin that would break out often and seemingly without reason. It was deeply frustrating as it felt like a reflection of how I was doing as a wife. So, in my desperation, I started trying out different laundry soaps. Even when we thought one was helping his skin, I would react to the smell of the laundry soap with headaches. We couldn't win. Soon, our first daughter was born, and I found out about all the baby branded cleaners and soaps, a whole other category to try out. But even our new little baby started having skin reactions.

When my mom noticed the bumps on my daughter's skin, she asked if I'd tried making my own laundry soap. I had never even heard of making my own! She showed me a few older recipes, and even recommended diluted vinegar for softener. I got to work shredding some gentle soap bars, mixing in borax and washing soda. Our clothes stopped smelling like a Yankee Candle store, our clothing was softer, and our skin cleared up. I was in shock. I started doing more research and reading labels. It didn't take me long to switch over more cleaning products to homemade versions. Here is a running list of some of the things we now make ourselves:

- Window cleaner = Diluted vinegar in a spray bottle
- Laundry soaps = Shredded bar soap, borax, and washing soda
- Spray disinfectant = Lemon-infused vinegar
- Drain unclogger = Baking soda in drain and washed down with vinegar
- Carpet cleaner = Baking soda sprinkled on carpet then vacuumed up
- Oven cleaner = Baking soda

Whether you hope to save some money with these tips or to see your health improve, you can't go wrong.

To do: Create your normal grocery list and then recreate the list with these categories: items you hope to preserve at home, things you can barter for, and things you will buy in bulk. Pray that God brings people into your life to trade and barter with, especially people whom you may have the opportunity to tell about God's great love.

Category	Grocery item

Day 3: Using What You Preserve

Wasting food is a big pet peeve of mine. So, what do I do when the freezer is full, and the jars are stacking up? How do I use up the bounty from the summer? If you remember chapter 3, day 4 when we put together the bags of freezer food by the month, that's a good place to start. You can also do the same thing with shelf foods. Instead of putting all your canned peaches in one area, you can split them up by month and use up each amount as you move forward.

Are you still stumped on how to use things? There are several websites that will take your list of items and create a unique meal plan for your family based on what you input. AI can be used for this too. You don't have to think it all up on your own. Here is an example:

Meats	3 lbs hamburger 3 (2-inch) pork steaks 1 pint bone broth
Vegetables	1 quart canned beans 1 pint canned carrots 1 cup frozen peas
Fruits	1 quart canned peaches
Fresh	5 lbs russet potatoes 3 sticks butter Milk Garlic
Staples	2 cups rice 2 cups flour

These grocery items can make nine meals for four people:

- Pork & Potato Stew
- Bean & Pork Soup
- Hamburger & Rice Skillet
- Grilled Pork Steak & Potatoes
- Bean & Rice Bowl
- Hamburgers with Rice & Peas
- Potato Cakes
- Shepherd's Pie
- Peaches & Biscuits

The last thing you want to do is take all this time to store up food and then never follow through with using it. Even preserved foods don't last forever—eventually, the quality will degrade. Proverbs 12:27 says, "The lazy man does not roast what he took in hunting, but diligence is man's precious possession." In Bible times you would need to roast, smoke, or dry your meat immediately after catching it since refrigeration was not an option. If a lazy man didn't follow through, the meat would go to waste. Similarly, harvesting your produce is only a piece of the pie; you also need to process it and finally eat it. Otherwise, you've wasted your time. If you make a habit of incorporating your preserved foods into your meals, you will gradually use up your supply and not waste the work you have done.

Here are some more unique ways to utilize your preserved goods:

- **Charcuterie boards:** So much potential for these snack trays. I love a spread of dried apple rings, nuts, pickled beets, fresh bread, cured sausage slices, homemade crackers, and fresh berries. My kids love it when I make an assortment of items to choose from while we play a board game as a family.
- **Relish roulette trays:** This is a fun one for gatherings. I'll take a little bit of each type of pickled items I have and

make a tasting bar to add to burgers and brats. I purposely don't label so that every bite is a unique surprise.

- **Fusion tacos:** Tacos are a weekly dinner at our house and making them unique has become an enjoyable challenge. You can mix relish with fresh finely sliced veggies like radish or cabbage to make a delicious new taco style and flavor.
- **Snack packs:** Mixing dried fruits and vegetables with homemade crackers or pretzels is great for on-the-go families.
- **Breads:** I like to add jam that didn't fully set to my sweet breads or add dried cherry tomatoes to a hearty savory bread.
- **Powders:** Any dried veggies like pumpkin or squash can get powdered to add to breads, soups, or dips for enhanced flavor and nutrition.
- **Dips:** Making a nice dip for bread or crackers or a spread for sandwiches is a great way to use dried or pickled items. My kids love to create their own unique blends using a sour cream base.
- **Sauces:** Our family loves curry and chutney. Both are a quick addition that add a fancy flair to any meal.
- **Soups:** There isn't much I can't put into a soup. From a tomato base to a rich broth, making soup with some fresh rolls is always a big hit.
- **Mocktails & popsicles:** A good kombucha mixed with fruit puree can make a wonderful drink after a hot day or a healthy popsicle for the kids.

I'd like to be abundantly honest that my family doesn't like everything that I make. I remember getting a great deal on ripe pineapple one year and taking the time to dry some, can some, and freeze some. I was so excited to have an "exotic" preserved food in my pantry when we live so far north. But when I made smoothies, the kids didn't like the texture. Then I tried to make a snack mix with peanuts and pineapple pieces, which they ate except for the pineapple. The canned pineapple was the only one they would eat, and only if I put it onto some homemade pizza. It was a frustrating experience, but now I know not to do much with pineapple at our house. I keep a notebook with recipes, and when things flop, I will make a note, or if it's a big hit, I'll add a little heart to indicate it's a family favorite.

To do: Take your pantry lists from yesterday and use them to create a custom meal plan for your family. If you have an abundance of certain preserved food, consider how you can use it to bless others through a bake sale or benefit. Think about whether you can use any of your saved goods for holiday gifts, too. Some of my favorite gifting options are homemade vanilla, quick breads, honey lollipops, and peanut brittle.

Day 4: Hospitality

If you've read much of your Bible you will know it's flooded with hospitality, from Abraham feeding angels, to Jesus providing at a wedding feast and feeding thousands in the desert. It may feel daunting to even think about filling your house with guests that may pass judgment on every misplaced crumb and over-seasoned bite. But trust me, it's so worth it.

In Hebrews 13:2 it says, "Do not forget to entertain strangers, for by doing so some have entertained angels." And 1 Peter 4:9 is even more direct saying, "Be hospitable to one another without grumbling." If we are going to be giving our homes to God with intentionality, we can't ignore this, even if it's uncomfortable. Even if your home is small. Even if you're messy. Even if you live in the middle of nowhere. Simply extending the invitation is all that God asks us. If you're afraid, ask God to give you boldness. Here are some tips that I use to make sure I have the capacity to be hospitable, even if it's the last minute:

- **Extra plates and cups:** I keep a stash of paper plates and disposable cups for extra guests because people are looking for presence and connection, not fine dining. On the flip side, for a fancier meal, on a high shelf is a dish set from my grandma that I can pull out and use with my other plates, because I know she'd love that.

- **Easy snacks or desserts:** Sometimes a whole meal isn't necessary. Sometimes a plate of crackers and cheese with a little bowl of homemade jelly is a perfect charcuterie. I often keep quick breads like zucchini in my freezer; it's easy to pop out and let it thaw to enjoy. This keeps my kitchen from getting messy but still has cozy homemade vibes.
- **Don't stress about the mess.** My house is lived in. There will be toys on the living room floor and crumbs under the table. I let people know, "Hey, it's a bit messy but I'd love to have you over for coffee if you don't mind." This is the opposite of a curated life online that people pretend to have. It's real, raw, and in the moment. It gives others permission to be and feel the same. So, embrace a lived-in home for all it has to give.
- **My go-to hospitality gift/snack is:** ....

If you are struggling for reasons to invite people over, here is my go-to list for our home. Feel free to add your own ideas to this:

- **Game nights:** Board games and charcuterie boards are a win every time.
- **Pool or beach day:** Take your hospitality on the road with a little cooler of snacks and plenty of time to listen.
- **Play dates with kids:** For some reason, two kids feels like ten and ten kids feels like two. When our kids play together, it gives us time to encourage one another.
- **Coffee/tea bar:** It's hard to say no to a warm beverage, especially with inflation rising prices at the take-out window.
- **Expertise help:** Need something sewn? I can do that. Need a car repair? Great, my husband gets home soon—come over and let him look at it while we talk about life. Applying for a new job and want a second look at that resume? Awesome, I'll do my best to help—here's a dessert while you wait for me to dust off that business degree from years ago.
- **My go-to invitation is:** ....

In an age of endless loneliness, this is the cure that Jesus gives. Jesus sends His Holy Spirit to dwell within us to make us His home. Ephesians 3:17b says, "that Christ may dwell in your hearts through faith . . ." It's no coincidence that when Jesus was born, He is called Emanuel, which means, "God with us." Be with people, even if you don't know what to say. Showing up is often enough, and the Holy Spirit will help you with the rest.

On Mother's Day one spring, we went to my mother-in-law's grave to clean it and plant flowers. It was a cool day, and even the breeze felt sad. Between all of us, the work went quickly, and we had a jug of water left over. My husband was about to dump it out when we noticed another lady working and planting around a grave not far away. I walked over and said hello with the intention of giving her the extra water for her flowers. She said hello and as soon as I saw the gravestone, I sat down next to her. It was for a toddler, her tiny son, and her eyes were full of tears. I didn't know what to say; I could only imagine how she felt. I simply helped her weed and held space with her. Was my water jug worth much? No. But it was the stepping stone I used to approach someone in grief. We prayed together that day and stayed in touch for a while. God uses even the smallest things to bring healing to others.

To do: Invite someone over that you don't know well. Pray over your home and ask God that He makes it a place of comfort and hope. Pray before they come and ask God to give you words to say and listening ears to hear.

Day 5: Composting

Composting involves taking what is wasted and rotten, what essentially has died, and allowing it to turn into something good over time. In the same way we wait for seeds to sprout, we wait for compost to become dirt. There are ways to speed this process up and ways to make it less intense work—it just depends on the type of composting you decide on. Here are five small scale methods to think about for your home.

1. **Backyard composting:** This is the most common way to compost. It's a bin or open pile that has a mix of kitchen scraps, leaves, and grass clippings. You can flip or turn the pile to speed up the process, or let it sit and decompose slowly.
2. **Bokashi composting**: This method uses microbes to decompose even the hardest things, like meat and dairy.
3. **Bin or tumbler composting:** Put your scraps, leaves, and grass into a large container. This is compact and tidy and keeps the animals out.
4. **Vermicomposting:** A fancy way to say a worm farm! Worms are hyper-efficient at turning compost into dirt. This can even be done inside your home with little effort or mess. Bonus: sell the worms for fishing as they multiply.
5. **Direct composting:** Take your bucket of scraps and bury it in your garden and let nature handle the rest. Pick a new spot each day.
6. **City-sponsored composting:** Some cities have composting options at the curb along with trash and recycling.

In Matthew 26, there is a beautiful recounting of Jesus being anointed with oil in preparation for His death. Some of the disciples said that the oil was wasted in this process. But with God, nothing is wasted, even if it may look that way to us. Just like Jesus reframes his anointing, we need to reframe how we think of death and what it can become over time. Paul explains this in Romans 8:13: "For if you live according to the flesh, you will die but if by the Spirit you put to death the deeds of the body, you will live." Through death, God makes things new in Him. Take a few minutes

and praise God for all the ways He has redeemed you and your old way of life and made it new.

Composting is a tricky subject at our home. I want to compost but my husband does not. He has valid concerns about smells, handling, and pest control—I get it. I want to compost for the garden benefits of helping our soil improve. This is also not the hill I want to die on. I explained my side of it and now if I want to improve my soil, my husband will gladly go pick up a load of composted manure instead of composting table scraps daily. These are the conversations and compromises that you will have to make as you decide what's best for your family. Don't be afraid to have those conversations so that your homestead is the best for your entire family.

To do: Research and consider starting a compost system. If you do start one, teach your family what to put in the compost and how it helps the soil improve over time. Talk about how God takes our broken lives and regenerates them through Jesus so we can live for Him to the fullest.

WEEK 5:
Animals

God is the master of all creation, and a big part of creation is the animals! If you're hoping to add animals to your homestead, then understanding what your options are is imperative. Some animals require more space, while others may not be allowed by your township zone. Pray over what God would have your home and family do as you expand.

Jesus himself is called the Good Shepherd. His sheep know His voice and obey Him. If you look online at videos, you can see this in action even today with sheep and shepherds. To take the time to have that kind of relationship with our animals is a big commitment, not to be made on a whim. No matter what animals you choose, be certain that God wants your family to care for them well, like He cares for us.

Day 1: Bats, Birds, Bees & Bugs

Starting our animal week with creatures that are not normally managed may seem odd, but these animals are the cornerstone of a dynamic outdoor space. God has created our world to work together in unity and acknowledging that bats, birds, and bugs make an impact is important.

Changing my mindset about what I consider a pest or even a plague is something I've been working on, especially when the mosquitoes start biting. When God rescued the Israelites from Egypt there was a series of

plagues. Each plague involved something that the Egyptians worshiped, and God used each one to show His mighty power. Flies, frogs, and locusts swarmed when God called them to, and under normal conditions all these animals have a good place. But when we fail to give God glory like the Egyptians did, we will see things get out of line.

Birds are an effective way to control bugs in an outdoor space. Adding habitat, nesting boxes, and water will encourage birds to move into your space and make it home. When I render my cow fat into tallow, I save all the crunchy bits and mix it with bird seeds. This makes our own suet cakes for winter, and nothing goes to waste.

Bats are like birds in controlling bugs, except they work at night, eating bugs by the thousands. Bat houses and watering spots are great for bringing more of these amazing animals into your space. Many trees rely on pollinators to be fruitful and some bats work like pollinators in this way, so the more the merrier, in my opinion.

Not that we want all the bugs gone, but natural control is way better than using pesticides to keep the garden from getting eaten up. There are many bugs that will work with your garden to keep it safe like ladybugs, dragonflies, praying mantises, and spiders. Spraying with pesticides kills all bugs, even pollinators like bees.

If you want to consider having honey on your homestead, think about planting enough flowering varieties of plants to support the bees, and encourage your neighbors to do the same in exchange for a small jar of honey each year. The equipment needs of honeybees is fairly high, and I encourage you to do thorough research before jumping into it.

There are several ways to help manage bug pests that may be getting out of control:

- **Manual removal:** My garden has the mulched layered method, and this leads to loads of bugs that thrive in leaf matter. My number one issue is slugs. To fight them off, I go out on a rainy day and manually pick them off my plants and toss them into the woods where they belong. If you go weak at the knees at the thought of that, then no worries, some people will use a little handheld vacuum to suck them up and then dump them in the chicken coop for a tasty treat.
- **A healthy garden:** The best defense against bugs is a healthy garden, and that starts way back at the beginning of this book with the soil and choosing plants that thrive in your area. Be in your garden often so you can catch outbreaks early before they become too big a problem. Using crop rotation will also help so that any bugs that may have left eggs in the soil from the prior year will hatch to a new plant variety instead.
- **Order good bugs:** I have a friend who orders ladybugs each year to help eat aphids off her prize rose bushes. Other good bugs you can order include praying mantises. You can also encourage good bugs to join your garden area by adding bug hotels around your space for them to nest in.
- **Row covers, fencing, and netting:** These options are great for larger pests like deer and birds. They put a barrier between the animals and the garden, keeping the produce safe.
- **Natural-ish sprays and killers:** There are a few options in this category that I've had good success with; however, they are my last resort.
    - **Diatomaceous earth (DE):** This is available at most feed stores and is, essentially, very spiky tiny sand that cuts bugs as they travel through it. It is very handy for keeping pests down in small animal pens.
    - **Neem oil:** An oil derived from an African tree that can be sprayed onto plants in the morning. Spray onto leaves, not onto produce,

and do so in two rounds ten days apart. This will kill most pests where you apply it.

- **Bug bags:** For invasive bugs like the Japanese Beetle, you can get bags to hang around your garden that attracts the bugs and then traps them inside.
- **Borax:** Not just for cleaning, a little sprinkle of this on top of an ant hive will cause the ants to die from the inside of the hive out. I use this for biting ants that have made a home too close to where my kids play.

When we moved into our latest home, we discovered a local population of fox families in the abandoned lot next to ours. It was amazing to watch the cubs grow and learn. It was also a huge bonus to our garden as they hunted the rabbits that are so fast at reproducing. Then the lot next door started to be maintained, and the fox family had to move out. That year we had multiple rabbit nests inside our garden. Baby bunnies were eating all our new plants, and while my toddlers squealed with joy chasing them, the damage was done. My garden did poorly and the next year we put up some short fencing early in the season to keep them at bay.

Having predators in your area can be good and bad. While the foxes helped manage our bunny problem, they also would snatch up my neighbor's free-range chickens. It's an ebb and flow. If your area is prone to predators, consider what you can and can't control as you search for balance. Sometimes a family dog (or goose!) is the answer for chasing off unwanted guests in the garden.

One of the best additions we've made to our home is a bird-watching station. We have a stand a few feet from our living room window. It holds bird seeds, homemade suet cakes (in the cold months), a hummingbird feeder (in the warm months), and a squirrel perch. We keep our bird identification book on the windowsill and check off the birds as we see them. On sunny Sunday afternoons, we even had a red-tailed hawk take a swoop at the squirrel on the feeder. It's a story my kids re-tell again and again.

To do: Research what bugs are helpful in your area, and consider installing a bug hotel, bird house, and bat house on your homestead. Perhaps make a bird-watching station outside one of your windows. Pray that God softens your heart to give Him the glory even among the mosquito bites.

Day 2: Chickens, Ducks & Turkeys

The taste and quality of home-raised chickens and eggs is incomparable to those of store-bought in my opinion. Once you see the color and taste the flavor you will agree. However, raising chickens is a big commitment. You will have to feed, clean up after, and provide space for each chicken. There are many varieties of chickens; some are specifically raised for meat while others provide stunning eggs in many colors. Turkeys are raised for meat (hello, Thanksgiving dinner), and ducks are often raised for both eggs and meat.

It is important to pay attention to what is allowed in your local area so that you don't get fined for violations. If you find out that the rules are not homestead friendly, you can attempt to change the rules through petitions or community involvement. Pray over whether it's a good use of your time and resources to fight the rules and pray that God provides a local farmer in the meantime who can supply your family with meat and eggs.

Bird Type	Time Commitment	Space Needs	Extras
Egg chickens	Lay eggs for 2–3 years, can live for up to 10 years, and don't lay in winter.	3–4 square foot coop space and 10 square foot outdoor space per chicken	Eat kitchen scraps and provide manure for gardens.
Meat chickens	6–12 weeks and do not recommend longer life due to breeding limits	2 square feet of pen space	Short-lived birds and less active.
Turkeys	16–20 weeks for meat and can live for up to 10 years	15 square foot roaming space per bird and a place to roost at night	Protective of other birds and provide large feathers.
Ducks	Lay eggs for 2–3 years, 8–12 weeks for meat, and can live for up to 8 years.	4–6 square feet of shelter space per bird and 16–24 square feet outdoor space	Can utilize pond space and protect property well.

If you've been around a broody hen, you know how protective she is of her chicks and eggs, putting her body as a shield between danger and her young. It's amazing to see such a small creature be so fearless. Psalms 91:4a says, "He shall cover you with His feathers, and under His wings you shall take refuge . . ." What a beautiful image of God's protection over our lives. Like a mother hen who will relentlessly peck at anyone who gets close to her eggs or chicks, God too keeps us close to Him and His care.

Growing up on a little hobby farm, we had rabbits, sheep, dogs, cats, horses, chickens, parakeets, and even a little fawn one spring, and it was always great fun to catch them when they got out by accident. One year we had a free-range white turkey, and he would strut around the barnyard keeping the peace with all the other birds. We named him Captain Tom. On occasion, Tom would even chase us kids out of the yard, and we all knew not to play games with him. All of us except the racoon. It was a calm night, and we knew a racoon was somehow getting into our chicken coop and stealing eggs. We'd set a live trap in hopes of catching and relocating the animal. But that night was different. Our fully grown male turkey faced off with the racoon and won. While it was a gruesome mess, it was also a testimony to the fierce protection some animals have over their homes.

If you like the protective aspect of having animals, consider geese and ducks, which have been "alarm" animals for centuries. They are vigilant and will swarm at intruders, making loud squawks and honks. Different than a dog but still highly effective. The biggest threat I've seen to this category of animal is owls. You may have different predators in your area, and it's worth learning about them to keep your flocks safe.

If your animal pens are in full sun, keeping animals from overheating is important. It's a good idea to put a fan in the chicken coop if it's not ventilated well. Another way to beat the heat for animals is to make them an "ice cake." You can use some fruit peels or kitchen scraps to make it more appealing, but essentially, we will freeze a brick of water in a silicone bread pan and then drop it into the water trough or duck pond. It helps lower the water temperature and gets the animals excited to peck at it to get the scraps first.

To do: Investigate your local laws and rules for your HOA, township, county, and state for having chickens, ducks, or turkeys at your homestead. Ask your neighbors what they think too so that you can keep peace with those nearest to you. Pray over the time and space needed to care for these animals well.

Day 3: Rabbits & Fish

Rabbits are a unique animal to raise for a few reasons. They provide meat and fur but are also small, need little space, make amazing manure, and are noise free, making them ideal for raising in suburban spaces. Although if the idea of butchering an animal is enough to make you queasy, then rabbits may not be the right choice for you. And that's okay! Getting to know what you do and don't want to do is what we are figuring out.

Even if butchering is not something you want to do, you may be able to use a local butcher to do this portion of the work and pay for processing. If you own any animals, whether for profit, food, or a pet, there will come a time of death. Having a family conversation about how animals can be both friends and food is a good idea. In Genesis 1:26, God gives dominion of creation and animals to humans to care for. This is not an excuse to abuse or overuse the world, but a call to care for and nourish it. If rabbits are right for you, then learning how to breed them is part of the process. Having baby bunnies on your homestead is so fun for kids!

Some of the best breed crosses for raising meat rabbits are:

- New Zealand × Californian – a popular cross because it combines fast growth rate, high meat yield, and hardiness in heat or cold.
- Flemish Giant × New Zealand – great for larger meat yield but a little slower to grow.

- Champagne d'Argent × Californian – a great balance of meat and valuable pelts.

Each of these types as a pure breed can also be wonderful on their own, depending on what your goals are.

If you're interested in rabbits but not in meat, there are other creative ideas to consider. Breeding for 4-H or other showing competitions is possible. Another thought is photo shoots with rabbits, especially around Easter, or a "Borrow a Bunny" or "Rent a Rabbit" business for birthday parties and other events. Rabbits are smart and friendly when trained, so keep an open mind as you think through homestead ideas.

Raising or stocking fish is also a great way to add protein to your homestead. Whether you decide to use a pond you have and "stock it" with fish to eat, or if you want to look into aquaponics, both are unique options if you have the resources. Aquaponics is a setup that utilizes water as the growing medium for plants instead of dirt. Adding fish into the water provides the nutrients the plants need to thrive. This is a complete circuit of sustainability, and the fish can be for eating or for the plants only.

Another option is to simply go fishing. Our area is full of local places to fish for all kinds of species that are good to eat. You will probably need a license to fish in your state so be sure to get one before fishing in a public water area. I am not blessed to live near the ocean, but if I did, then using the bounty found there would also be on my list of homesteading activities. Some fish that are easy to order in large quantities are:

- **Bluegills:** Good to eat for both people and larger fish.
- **Largemouth bass:** Big fish and easy to catch.
- **Hybrid sunfish:** Easy to catch and process due to size and shape.
- **Tilapia:** Good to eat and easy to process.

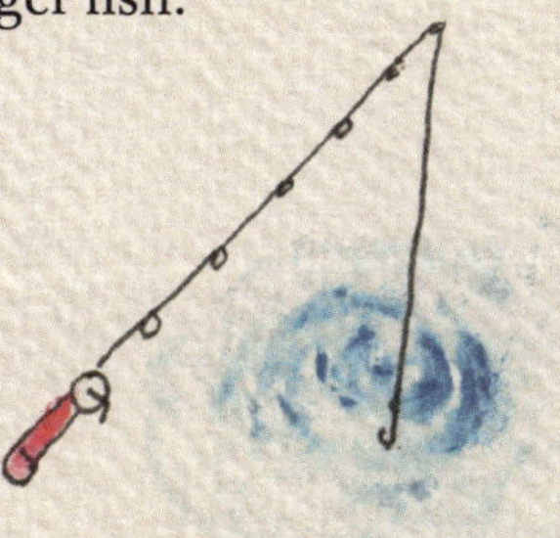

I grew up fishing and eating what we caught. To this day, getting some time to fish is one of my favorite ways to spend the day. Once we went way up north, nearly to Canada, on a family vacation. We decided to hike out to a super clear lake and carry canoes with us; it was so beautiful and the lake so deep. I took my fishing pole and wondered what kinds of fish I might catch. It didn't take long for something to grab my bait, and for the first time in my twelve years of life, I wondered if I'd caught something bigger than I was.

As the water churned and the fish came closer to the surface, I could see the jaws of a huge pike. Where we are, this is as close to a shark encounter as we can get. I looked at the pike and he looked at me and with one giant flip he broke my line and was gone. I was so disappointed. My dad walked over to remind me that just because one opportunity gets away doesn't mean you should stop casting out your line to try again. So, if you try some of these homestead ideas and they don't work out, don't be too upset—you can always give it another go or pick something else to try.

To do: Pray and have a family discussion about death, focusing on how Jesus died for us and rose again. Talk about how death is not the end and how God loves His creation even through the redemption process. This may be hard for children to understand, depending on their ages, so pray for wisdom as you work through complex feelings with your family.

Day 4: Large Animal Meats & Fats

I don't know if there are many farm animals cuter than a highland cow but considering I'm working with less than an acre of land and I'm inside our city limits, I will have to be content with dreaming of owning one. I had to tell my kids no to horses, too. Knowing your local rules may make your choices in this category limited. Sometimes rules will change if your neighbors complain or dislike what you want to do. Ask God first through prayer about what kind of commitment you can honestly make, as bigger animals take more time, space, and feed. The benefits can also be wonderful for your family and community.

If you're in the same boat as I am and can't have large animals at your home, then look for a local farmer or homesteader who sells beef, sheep, goat, or buffalo. You will pick up these meats, usually already frozen and labeled, in either freezer paper or vacuum sealed. Look for pricing based on these measurements for buying beef:

- **Pound:** Most stores sell meat by the pound and farmers will, too. However, it usually costs slightly more than buying in larger quantities and will often be limited to ground beef.
- **Quarter:** About 100–130 pounds of packaged meat in mixed cuts, with the majority being in ground beef. You will need 4–5 cubic feet in your freezer to fit all this.
- **Half:** Literally half of the cow in mixed cuts of both sides of the cow, usually about 200–260 pounds of meat. You will need 8–10 cubic feet in your freezer to fit all this.

- **Whole:** Literally the whole cow, cut by request, ground, and packaged. You will need 16–20 cubic feet in your freezer to fit all this.
- **Extras by request:** Suet/fat, organ meats, tongue, ox tail, and soup bones. There may be a small fee to package these additional items, but they are worth getting if you like to make broth, tallow products, or enjoy organ meats (liver, heart, etc.).

In the Bible, there are many who raise flocks, including Jacob and Laban in Genesis 30:31–43. Jacob wanted to leave Laban's service, since he had paid the dowry to marry his daughters. But Laban wanted him to stay because he knew God was blessing him through Jacob's care of his goats and sheep. So, they made a deal. Jacob's pay would be all the goats and sheep that were spotted, brown, or striped, and Laban would own the solid-colored animals, which was the vast majority. Laban jumped at the deal, knowing how spots and dark colors were rare in his flocks. But God had a plan to protect Jacob and his interests.

Laban separated the flocks by color and space to keep Jacob trapped and away from his herds. But Jacob had learned how to breed health and strength into the flocks over his years of shepherding. He knew that certain trees had an impact on healing, reproduction, and strength as part of how God created them. Science has shown this now that we have the ability to analyze the herbal properties of plants. Jacob could, in fact, use these trees to create more fertility and healthier animals as they bred. Jacob kept his part of the deal by tending to the flocks well, even though Laban continued to try to cheat him, and so God blessed the flocks with speckles, browns, and spots in each new batch of babies until Laban became angry with Jacob and let him leave with his family and herds. The takeaway for me in this story is that Jacob did his job well and God made sure to bless him, even when others were out to harm him. When we follow what God says and work hard, God tends to bless and protect. He will do the same for you if you continue to put God first in your home and life. We may still encounter trials and even tragedy, but we can trust that God is with us through it all.

If you're looking to get multiple animal types, consider pasture rotations as part of your homestead plan. This encourages soil regeneration and lets all animals get a bit of pasture time as they grow. If you don't have acreage dedicated to pasture, that's okay too—you can purchase hay (dried and bundled grass mixture) to feed your flocks as they grow. Be aware that hay and straw are not the same thing. Straw is the bundled stems of harvested wheat, barley, etc. and has no nutrition content for the animals, though it's good for bedding and nesting boxes.

Here is a breakdown of what an average animal eats per day so you can calculate if you have enough to raise what you'd like to raise.

Animal	Ratios	Example
Cows	Need about 2.5% of their body weight in dry feed per day. If your feed has water content, you will need to account for that as well.	A 1,000-pound cow × 2.5% = 25 pounds of dry feed. Grass hay has 8% water content, which adds another 2 pounds to the total = 27 pounds.
Pigs	Need about 4% of their body weight per day, more if it's below freezing.	A 100-pound pig × 4% = 4 pounds of feed per day.
Sheep	Need about 3% of their body weight per day.	A 100-pound sheep × 3% = 3 pounds of feed per day.
Goats	Need 3% of their body weight per day unless they are being milked, then they need 7%.	A 100-pound goat who is being milked × 7% = 7 pounds of feed per day.

We personally don't have large animals at our homestead, but my father-in-law does. This gives us an opportunity to help and access some of the produce. One of the main things we use is the suet from the cows. Over time I've been able to create a little business around tallow products in my county. In the next section, we will talk more about how to monetize your homestead, but for now, keep looking for the things God has blessed you with and for ways to use them uniquely.

To do: When we are faithful to the job that God has called us to, there is no limit to the blessings He can give. This doesn't mean God has to bless us, but often He does. Pray over whether you should buy or raise larger meat animals.

Day 5: Dairy

Dairy is so much more than cows. It includes goats, cheese, lotion, soap, kefir, loads of laws, and plenty of superstition. If you've been a part of the homestead community for any amount of time, I'm sure you've seen the arguments for and against raw milk. Honestly, I'm not here to convince you one way or another. I will, however, lay out some of the pros and cons so you can decide for yourself what you'd like for your family.

Item	Pros	Cons
Raw milk: Milk that is not subjected to heat or straining of fats prior to consumption.	Nutrition content, probiotics, lactose digestion, taste, freshness, unprocessed, and more natural.	Possibility of contamination and foodborne illness, lack of scientific research, legal restrictions, and short shelf life.
Pasteurized milk: Milk that has been heated to kill off bacteria and been separated from fats.	Sterilized all bad bacteria, increased shelf life, lower risk of contamination.	Removed vitamins and good bacteria, altered taste and texture.
Homemade cheese: Cheese made at home using any type of milk and rennet.	Higher nutrition, fewer additives, cost effective, personalized taste, and connection to nature.	High time commitment and equipment needs, takes skill to do correctly.
Homemade milk soaps & lotions: Items made with milk as a base ingredient	Natural ingredients, personal customization, and lower carbon footprint.	Time, effort, harder to control quality, harder to find ingredients if not raised yourself.
Kefir: Fermented milk drink	Rich in probiotics, good for bone and heart health, and helps control blood sugars.	Allergic reactions to lactose, alcohol content, infection risk for immune compromised.
Yogurt: Made with any type of milk subjected to low heat over time with a starter culture and sugar.	Ingredient control, personalized flavors, and higher probiotic content.	Time-consuming, equipment needs, and risk of contamination.

Every state has its own laws and regulations around raw milk, its consumption, and its salability. In my state, I cannot legally buy raw milk. Instead, I need to purchase a cow share, meaning I pay to care for a cow and get a portion of its produce in exchange. I must sign an agreement with the farmer and keep my information up-to-date with them. It's not convenient or easy, but for us it's worth it. I also buy regular milk from the store; we are not exclusive. Do what's right for your family.

Milk has long been used in the Bible as a measure of blessing, as the promised land to the Israelites is described as "flowing with milk and honey." It's no accident that in 1 Peter 2:2 it says to ". . . desire the pure milk of the word, that you may grow thereby." Milk is known for being able to nourish and revitalize. As a mother, I've seen this as I feed my babies. Take a moment to think about the last time you were able to be nourished by God's words. Thank God for His willingness to bring us His inner peace and encouragement when we stay hydrated by the Bible.

To do: Look up the laws in your state regarding raw milk. Discuss with your family whether owning an animal for milking is right for you; if so, decide if it's a short- or long-term goal. If you want to consume it but not have the animal, then look at local farmers for the potential of purchasing raw milk.

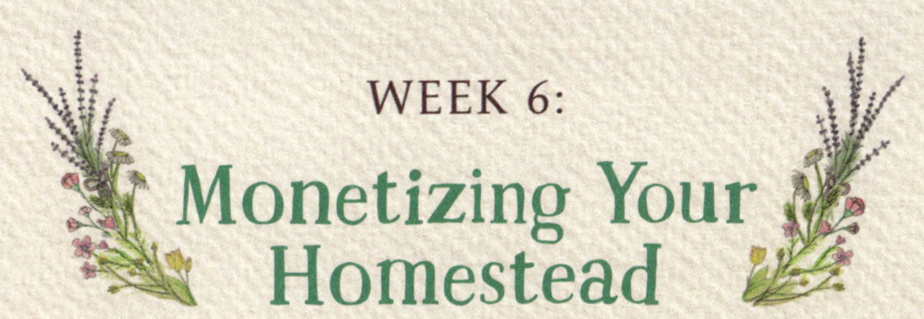

WEEK 6:

Monetizing Your Homestead

A few chapters ago, I was honest when I said that creating a homestead would not be financially efficient but would benefit your quality of life. If you want to help with the budget side of things, then by using your skills, knowledge, and time you can bring in some extra money to help offset the costs. I want to be very clear that God does not promise financial blessings in this life; He promises His presence through the Holy Spirit, which is the ultimate blessing. So even if you pray all the prayers, do all the giving, and be kind to everyone, there is no promise of financial success by the world's standards. The spiritual benefits will be great even if the worldly benefits don't match up.

If you feel called to contribute to your family financially, or to the community with sharing information, or with your church through the food pantry, or whatever it may be, listen to God's call and follow it. That is where the true blessings will be found, in surrender and obedience.

Day 1: Cottage Food Laws & Giving

If you've never heard of cottage food laws, then this may be a bit surprising. You can't just sell food any way you want; you have to follow rules. If you just groaned slightly, I get it. It feels like the government gets to meddle with everything these days. There are some laws that keep people safe and others that are the result of lobbying and bureaucracy. Every state has its own set of cottage food laws and some are stricter than others.

You will need to pray over which things you agree with and don't agree with. In Titus 3:1 it says, ". . . to be subject to rulers and authorities . . ." Be careful not to dismiss a law that God has established through an authority, but also weigh that with godly love and service. For example, in my state it's against the law to sell beverages out of your home. This law was made to prevent anyone with a natural water spring from bottling and selling water and thus depleting the land of its natural water supply. But I grow elderberries which, when mixed with other spices and raw honey, make a powerful healing beverage. Technically, I could get in trouble selling it, but I also want my friends and family to be healthy. So instead, I dry the ingredients and make a dry mix kit. I can honor the law by not selling a beverage and honor God's law of helping others by making a dry kit. Pray over the laws in your state. Ask God to give you a creative mindset to abide by both God's laws and man's laws.

Other common laws include labeling rules. Often you will have to create an ingredient list for crafted products. Usually, ingredients are listed from highest to lowest content, and labels also include weight, price, and expiration date. For example, a label for a loaf of sourdough bread could look like this:

Sourdough Bread
Exp 4/10 1 Pound $10.00
Flour, Sourdough Starter, Water, Salt, Yeast, Sugar

The goal with labeling is to protect the consumer from allergies, and you from a lawsuit. Using free programs like Canva and a thermal label printer will help you create good labels that don't add too much to the cost of your product. If you'd rather avoid all the computer-based things, you can also write a label by hand and attach it to your product with some thread. Do what you prefer and keep it simple, so you don't get overwhelmed.

If your state requires you to have a commercial kitchen, it can be a hard stop for your baking business. I've found the best work-around for this is

that most larger churches have a commercial kitchen already set up and will often rent it out. Keep that in mind when you read through the rules in your state. In my state, I have to put a note on my products that says it was created in a home kitchen and give them my address.

If you've found that the laws are over-restrictive, there is another work-around that can be used, called a "farm share." Similar to a cow share, this allows people to subscribe to your homestead for a monthly fee. In return, they receive a portion of your abundance on the farm, and you get money to continue your efforts. It will mean you have to create a contract for your customers and keep track of whom you sell to.

If none of this seems like the right path for you, no worries. You can always make things and gift them to others. Gift giving is something that God is so good at. It says in James 1:17 that "every good and perfect gift is from above, and comes down from the Father of lights, with whom there is no variation or shadow of turning." Your gifts are a reflection of God's great capacity to give and an act of love. On the flip side of that, making an income at what God has blessed you with is not wrong. In Proverbs 31:24 it says, "She makes linen garments and sells them, and supplies sashes for the merchants." The woman described in these verses is faithful to God and her family through her work and is blessed because of it. This choice is between you and God.

To do: Research the cottage food laws and pray over what God would want you to sell. Ask God to make your abundance a blessing to others that leads them back to Him. If making money is far from your thoughts, then pray about how you can create gifts for others instead. Pray that God gives you a heart for generosity.

Day 2: What to Sell

If you're wondering how many zucchinis you need to sell to fund next year's seed purchase, it's a lot. Thankfully, there are many great ways to earn income that are beyond veggies (although veggies are wonderful). Here is a breakdown of some ideas to consider that take into account time involved, investment to start, and difficulty. In the next chapter we will consider *where* to sell; today we will focus on *what* to sell.

Idea	Time	Investment	Difficulty
Animals: Rabbits, goats, etc.	Breeding of animals and gestation periods	Low if animals are owned, higher if breeding stock is needed	Easy to Medium
Baked Goods: Rolls, breads, sourdough, etc.	Baking times	Low. Kitchen supplies and ingredients	Easy
Bouquets: This can be flower, or even veggie or mushroom bouquets	Planting, caring for, cutting, and arranging will be a four-season commitment	Low start cost depending on the type of flowers planted	Easy to Hard

Idea	Time	Investment	Difficulty
Classes: teaching skills, foraging, or animal care	Preparing class materials, space, and advertising	Low. A printout or basic supplies, can be done online.	Easy to Hard
Compost: By the bag or load, or kits	Byproduct of animals and time	Low. Ways to move or package it.	Easy
Crafts: Knitting, crochet, jewelry, cards, etc.	Depends on size of project, difficulty, and experience	Supplies purchase (varies depending on craft)	Easy to Hard
Dairy: Milk, butter, cheese	Care for animals and milking daily. Or buying milk and processing.	High. Animal care and equipment to process.	Hard
Dried herbs	Growing plants	Seeds or starters—some will return every year. Dehydrator options.	Easy
Eggs	Care for chickens	Medium for care of hens.	Easy
Fruits: berries, apples, etc.	Planting and growing times depend on plant.	Low. Picking baskets.	Easy
Hay/Straw: Bales or rolls	Planting, cutting, and bailing	High. Tractor and bailer equipment.	Medium to Hard
Honey	Care for bees	Higher for equipment needed to spin honey.	Medium to Hard
Maple Syrup	Tapping trees and cooking down sap	Low to High. Pans for cooking down and tapping equipment. Larger scale "sugar shacks" cost more.	Medium
Meat: Smoked, frozen, etc.	Animal care and processing	High. Land and barn space, milking equipment.	Medium to Hard
Mushrooms	Once started only minimal effort is needed	Low. Start with a kit or a few fresh logs.	Easy
Pet treats	Baking times	Low. Kitchen supplies and ingredients.	Easy

(*Continued . . .*)

Idea	Time	Investment	Difficulty
Photography space rental (renting your property out for photo shoots)	Depends on how rugged or planned you want to make the spaces.	Medium – Maintained curated space for photos, insurance, and time to coordinate with photographer.	Medium
Preserves: Jam, jelly, pickles, etc.	Picking and preserving	Low to medium. Canning supplies & equipment	Easy to Medium
Retreats & conferences	Organizing, sourcing speakers, and marketing	High. Location to host, serve food, and/or stay overnight.	Hard
Soaps & lotions	Flexible with times and amount involved	Low. Can get started with a kit.	Easy
Starter plants & seeds	Time planting and watering	Low for plant trays and seeds. Medium for greenhouse.	Easy to Medium
Tallow & lard	Either care and processing of animals and/or purchasing suet to render	Low if buying raw fats or high if raising own animals.	Easy to Hard
Teas	Growing plants	Seeds or starters—some will return every year. Dehydrator options.	Easy to Medium
Textiles: Clothing, quilts, etc.	Depends on size of the project, difficulty, and experience	Sewing machine and supplies	Easy to Medium
Vegetables	Time planting, watering, weeding, and harvesting	Low. Seeds or starter plants.	Easy
Woodworking: Bird feeders and houses, bat boxes, butterfly houses, décor, etc.	Depends on size of project, difficulty, and experience	Medium. Woodworking tools and supplies.	Medium
Worms: fishing	Compost byproduct	Low. Large Tupperware bins for vermiculture, or collect worms from nature.	Easy

Are you seeing the creativity in some of these ideas? God loves creativity. From His own creative works to those He inspires us with. When we create, we are mimicking our creator. When God made His plans to build the tabernacle tent under Moses, He went out of his way to prepare and select craftsmen to work on His temple. Exodus 36:2 says, "Then Moses called Bazalel and Aholiab, and every gifted artisan in whose heart the LORD had put wisdom, everyone whose heart was stirred, to come and do the work." God wanted it to be beautiful and functional. God cared about the whole project from start to finish. As crafters and creators, I think we have all felt that "stirring." Inspiration compels us to create; it's a gift from God to be used for His glory.

What was the purpose of the temple? First, to bring Him glory and a place for His people to come and glorify Him. Second, it was a place to offer sacrifices to mitigate sins. Third, it collected income to support the priests and the poor. Similarly, we honor and glorify God in our home and bodies. Our relationship with Jesus removes our sins. Our work supports our family and lets us be generous to the poor and to our churches.

For our family, the answer came in the middle of some desperate prayers to provide extra income to keep our kids in Christian school. I'd prayed this prayer every year it seemed, and God always showed up by giving my husband a little raise or a side bonus or something that just covered the amount we needed. What I wasn't expecting was God tapping me to do something more.

It was a normal playdate with some amazing moms who also love Jesus. I offered them some of my homemade tallow lotion. They raved about it, so, I gave them some to take home. Then they told others, so I made another batch and decided to offer it for a price. God sold that batch out within a week. I stayed after school letting the kids play as I offered up my prayer for providing again in my head and heart. Then the two friends who took a jar home that first playdate walked over to me and asked, "Why are you still praying? It looks like God's providing. When are you making another batch?" I swear I had the deer-in-headlights look in my eyes. I couldn't see it at first. God is continuing to provide in this way again and again for my family. He can do the same for you with whatever blessing or skill that God has gifted you with. Just because it's easy for you doesn't mean it is to others. Or maybe it's not easy. Maybe God is asking you to stretch in new ways to bring blessings to others and your family. If so, He will equip you along the way.

To do: Ask God to make it clear if He wants you to monetize your homestead. Understand that the answer may be "not now," and that's alright too. Waiting on God's timing is always the best choice. If the answer is yes, start brainstorming ideas.

Day 3: Where to Sell

When it came to selling my tallow lotion, I quickly realized selling to moms at the school pickup line was only going to get me so far. I needed to have my own location to sell from. So, I spent that early spring building a small farmstand off the back of my garden shed near the road. It may sound daunting to build a new structure, but there are a lot of possibilities that are manageable. Pinterest is full of adorable farmstands made from old TV cabinets and other things that take much less time and work than what I chose to do. My farmstand was a way to use up lumber from our house renovation and other miscellaneous materials we had lying about the yard. Is it perfect? Not at all. But I had so much fun putting it together.

Once summer came, I started selling my lotions, jams, and extra vegetables at the roadside stand and marketing it through Facebook. It kind of worked. I live in a poor, rural area, so I realized quickly that local customers wanted things cheap and cared less about aesthetics than I did. As the days turned cold, I had to remove my items so they wouldn't freeze, and I was back to selling them after school again. I needed another idea.

Next, I tried out a craft market on a cold spring Saturday right before Easter. I did make some money, but what I didn't expect was the toll it took on my family with me being gone that whole day to set up, sell, and take down. Moreover, my husband wasn't a fan, and his vote matters to me. On to the next idea. I tried selling exclusively through Facebook Marketplace. It worked ok, but it became clear that people did not like having to drive so far into the country to pick things up, and I didn't want to make regular trips to different towns each week either. At that point, I went back to praying and asking God what He wanted me to do, because clearly my ideas weren't working like I thought they would. I prayed for two weeks for God to show me His ideas, not mine.

Then, out of the blue, a lady from evening church approached me and said, "Hey, my mom owns a vendor market and there isn't anyone selling tallow there. Would you want to have a small booth to try?" My heart soared, and I wondered if this was what God wanted. So, I said yes to a three-month test run. I posted my new location on social media and made a profit in my first month. I kept praying and asking God, where next? He opened other doors, and I prayed over each one. In fact, the only location I didn't pray over is the one that failed. God wants our hearts above all.

Here are some potential places to sell your homestead goodies:

- **Roadside stand:** Low overhead and costs to run. Easily customizable. Subject to theft if not careful.
- **Farmers market:** Usually a weekly event where you can connect with other vendors and sell to those who stop in.
- **Co-op, food shares & pantries:** A curated list of customers who receive your goods in exchange for a monthly subscription.
- **Vendor markets:** Curated and more for homemade items and goods than for fresh produce.
- **Online:** Easy to start selling through listings but requires good photos, internet, and the capacity to meet up with others or to ship goods.

In Matthew 21:12, Jesus visited the temple and found merchants selling goods and making money. He was filled with righteous anger and drove them out. It's not that Jesus is against making money or doing business, but He does care about where our hearts are in the process. Those businesses should have been doing the selling outside the temple, not inside it. Inside the temple is for the worship and glory of God. Moreover, their selling was taking up the place Gentiles could worship, and they were overcharging people, especially the poor. All of these practices go against what God calls us to do. So, regardless of a business going well or not, be sure that you keep Jesus at the center of your heart in the process, and don't let the money, stress, or work of selling take the place of Christ in your heart.

To do: Do any of these ideas stand out to you? It's okay to start small. It's okay to try a few things and see how they work for you.

Make a list of places you could sell near you. Find out if a roadside stand is permitted in your neighborhood. The important part is to pray over every business choice you make because God is in the details. Also, ask your family what the best fit for them would be as you pursue your goals.

Day 4: Tracking It All

In most states, any income that exceeds a certain amount is subject to taxes. While this may sound frustrating, Jesus made it clear in Luke 20:25 to "Render therefore to Caesar the things that are Caesar's, and to God the things that are God's." We are not to try to evade taxes or get upset, because God is ultimately in control. In Matthew 17:27, Jesus sent Peter to go fishing, and inside the fish's mouth was a coin to pay the temple taxes. Jesus did a miracle to cover the tax, but Peter still had to put in the work of fishing. Fishing was what they were good at, and Jesus used their skills for the benefit of His kingdom work; He wants to do the same with us.

Here are some spreadsheets you may want to get started to help keep your new venture organized. I am not a tax professional, so please consult with yours when you decide to try your hand at this. The laws change often, so be sure you keep an eye on them.

- **Budget:** This is a plan for your money that you create and then follow. Using a budget for your whole home is important, and doing one for your business is essential, too.
- **Income:** Farmstand income, class income, services income, market income, vendor income, book income.
- **Expenses:** Booth fees, supplies, animal costs, feed costs, equipment purchases.
- **Write-offs:** Phone cost, internet cost, home office space, harvest room storage space.
- **Customer information:** If you are doing a farm share or want to reach out to potential repeat customers, then keeping names, addresses, and contact information will be important.
- **Prayer requests:** When I had a farm stand, I made it a point to have a spot to leave prayer requests, and I dedicated some time each Sunday night to pray for each one. This has been one of the most rewarding parts of selling for me.
- **Time:** Keeping an account of how much time you spend on things will help you better price your items. For example, if it takes four hours to crochet that stuffed animal and you sell it for $40, then you are only paying yourself $10 an hour minus material expenses.
- **Debt:** The Bible says in Proverbs 22:7b that, "The borrower is servant to the lender." If your family is struggling with debt, consider trying to get out of more debt by choosing to not borrow more and/or to start paying down what you already have. I can tell you, the peace that comes from no debt is incredible and something I hope you experience.
- **Cost cutting:** This is a fun way to find out what kind of money you can save by doing things more economically or efficiently. For example, I put our clothes to dry on a laundry line when I can instead of using my gas dryer. This saves me a few dollars each week. It doesn't seem like much, but after a whole year it adds up.

Now that you have an idea of what to track, let's circle back to the Bible and give one more example of using skills to earn money. You may think that if you're praying for others, selling Bible products, and telling as many people as possible about Jesus then you *deserve* to be paid well and to be well provided for. This is the mindset of some missionaries and church staff that I know, unfortunately.

Thankfully, Paul has loads to say about it in 2 Thessalonians 3:7–12, where Paul points out that when he visited them and told them about Jesus, he didn't take advantage but spent time working (other parts of the Bible tell us Paul was a tentmaker by trade) and earning money for food and lodging so he would not be a burden to anyone. As an apostle, Paul has every right to ask to be provided for, but he chooses not to in order to set an example of the right heart posture for each of us. So, it's not about whether or not you make money, but where your heart is at during all of it.

To do: Start tracking things as you move forward with your homestead, even if it's for your own reference later and not for financial reasons. Pray over your finances with your spouse and talk about what your goals are for the future. Remember, we are stewards of the resources God has entrusted us with and He will want an account of how we used our resources for His glory.

Day 5: Tithing & the Lord of the Harvest

What is a tithe? By definition, it is a tenth of all increase. By design, it's a heart posture of acknowledging that all we have and are belongs to God. It's to demonstrate that we understand who is in control and where all blessings come from. The first mention of a tithe is when Abraham returned from a battle and gave a tenth to the Priest Melchizedek (Numbers 18:21–26 and Hebrews 7:1–9) and Abraham was blessed. Later on, the tithe was established as part of the temple and the Levites pay for being priests. While we no longer live under the Old Testament laws, we do still honor the same God and heart of it.

Jesus uses the example of harvest in Matthew 9:36–38. It says, "But when He saw the multitudes, He was moved with compassion for them, because they were weary and scattered, like sheep having no shepherd. Then Jesus said to His disciples, 'The harvest truly is plentiful, but the laborers are few. Therefore, pray to the Lord of the harvest to send out laborers into His harvest.'" As gardeners, we all understand how important it is to harvest things at the right time. Not too early or it could be tasteless, not too late or it could be rotten. As caretakers of animals, we understand that farm animals without a caretaker quickly become distressed and in need.

Jesus is putting both these thoughts together and asking His disciples to pray with Him for more workers, more disciples. Can you imagine how the disciples felt when Jesus told them to pray? My response would've been something like, "You're God. Can't you just call in the favor? Why do I need to pray?" I think the answer is in the verse before when Jesus looked and felt compassion.

When we pray to God, it is for our benefit, not God's. God knows what's going on. He does not need our play-by-play recap. He is using prayer to adjust our hearts. Jesus wanted the disciples, and us, to pray for more workers because it would make us see and acknowledge the state of those around us—our neighbors, our friends. Look around at how many people you know who are fighting anxiety, loneliness, and depression. They are weary and scattered, and we have the solution in Jesus. But are we going out to bring them to Jesus, or sitting back and watching from our safe homes where we have all we need? Prayer moves us to compassion, and compassion moves us to pray.

I write this with a deep sense of conviction, knowing that I've used my home as a fortress instead of a haven so many times. The disciples weren't to pray this prayer from the sidelines. They were with Jesus, actively helping in the harvest, and then asked to pray for more helpers, more disciples. So, before I pray to God to "send someone," I need to first look at my own feet and see where I'm standing. Am I in the harvest field working? Or on the hedgerow snacking on berries while others work. Because if it's the hedgerow, then those workers in the field are praying that I join them while I'm praying that God sends the person behind me out first.

As we near the end of this book, it's essential that we are still seeking God's kingdom, even from our homesteads. The goal is not to build a fence to keep the world out but to build a kitchen table big enough to invite as many to join us as we possibly can. It's to have family devotions that teach our kids to be fearless harvesters and seekers of lost sheep. It's hard work to harvest in the heat, sweat, and dirt—you'll be sore from the exertion. It's dangerous to seek out lost sheep that have gotten stuck in mud and thorns;

getting them out will leave some bruises and scars. It's worth it, though, to join Jesus in the harvest field and in the search for the sheep.

When I look at a holy homestead, I see a home that seeks to honor God and family. A place that invites those outside to a table of peace. A garden that grows in love for others with veggies and hugs. Animals that encourage a lifetime of compassion and care. A heart that says no to fear because our hope is rooted in Jesus. A holy homestead is joy in everyday creation and the invitation to taste and see that the Lord is good, His mercies are new every day. I pray that this is your heart as well.

To do: Consider giving a tithe to your church as part of your budget or a tithe of your homestead items to charity. Pray that God gives you a heart of generosity and thankfulness even when things are tight or hard.

CONCLUSION:

The Proverbs 31 Woman, a Homesteader

As we wrap up this book, I want to return to Proverbs 31. As I mentioned in the introduction, I've read this so many times in the past and felt that I have not measured up. However, reading it lately, all I can see is a woman of God who is using her home to honor God through homesteading. Walk with me as we dive into these verses and realize we can do this work and be a virtuous wife, even in today's world, without "doing it all."

Proverbs 31:10–31

Proverbs 31:10 "Who can find a virtuous wife? For her worth is far above rubies."

If God values this woman, then I definitely want to be like her, but it seems like such a high bar to reach. If you're comparing right now like I am, then know that being like Jesus is the ultimate goal and there is not a comparable passage for men in the Bible. Don't get too stuck right here because we need to dig a little deeper to understand.

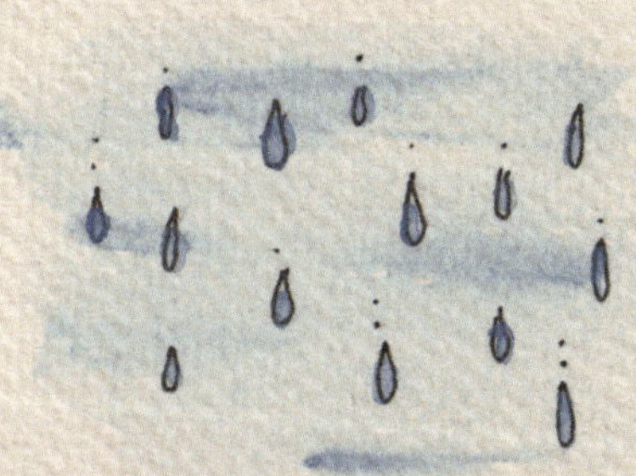

Takeaway: Women are valuable to God.

Proverbs 31:11 "The heart of her husband safely trusts her; So he will have no lack of gain."

The first quality that this woman has is trustworthiness. How many of us run the errands, tend to the home, get the groceries, make sure everything is as it should be? Your husband trusts you to handle these so he can focus on his job, or whatever God has called Him to do. This is God acknowledging that running a home is not easy, and it makes me feel seen in all the moments when I feel like no one notices all my efforts. God sees my work and knows its value. When God created Eve, he called her a "helper." This is the same word used to describe the Holy Spirit. What a calling we have as women of God!

Takeaway: God values trustworthiness.

Proverbs 31:12 "She does him good and not evil. All the days of her life."

As a wife, I could sabotage so much of my husband's life. I could set him up to fail. But I don't because I love him and want him to win. If you're at a place in your relationship where it's hard to do him good, then you need to take that to God. Not as a "you're in trouble" type way but to ask God to change your heart and fix what's broken in your marriage. God is our redeemer; He will redeem your situation as much as He does your soul. Consider marriage counseling if you feel things are rough.

Takeaway: Our heart place leads to our actions.

Proverbs 31:13 "She seeks wool and flax, and willingly works with her hands."

Now we know what kind of homestead this woman has. Wool is used for making clothing, and in ancient times had the reputation for being protective, pure, and associated with authority. Flax was valuable because it can be made into oil, rope, twine, linen, sailcloth, bandages, and oilcloth (a waterproof fabric). All the things needed for a merchant ship in the next verse, and highly sought out for trading.

Takeaway: She isn't doing everything; she is focused on a few key areas.

Proverbs 31:14 "She is like the merchant ships, she brings her food from afar."

Now that we understand the importance of flax, it makes more sense that she is compared to a merchant ship. She makes items used for travel and therefore has access to exotic foods from afar. This would often mean spices and herbs that would be beneficial for medicine and caring for her family.

Takeaway: She is caring for her family in the ways that God has led her to.

Proverbs 31:15 "She also rises while it is yet night, and provides food for her household, and a portion for her maidservants."

I don't know about you, but I am not an early riser. I'd prefer to sleep in. But what I can say is that when my children need me at night, I am instantly awake. I want to help them. Back in ancient times, for food to be ready for the next day, getting up at night to knead the dough and bake it would be essential. Remember, there were no refrigerators or bread machines. What it is getting at here is that she manages her time well for the benefit of those in her house.

Takeaway: Time management is important.

Proverbs 31:16 "She considers a field and buys it; From her profits she plants a vineyard."

Now that she has figured out the best way to handle wool and flax, she takes her profits and puts them to good use. She doesn't buy luxurious clothes or take an expensive trip; she instead reinvests it into her home by buying some land and building a vineyard. She's adding a new skill and doing it slowly over time without going into debt. Vineyards in those days were easy to rent out and collect from without having to be there daily, so this was a wise choice for her time and an easy way to make side money.

Takeaway: Go slow, master each area, and the next thing won't feel so daunting.

Proverbs 31:17 "She girds herself with strength, and strengthens her arms."

At first glance it sounds like this woman works out. But it's deeper than just being strong. To "gird" means to prepare for action or to add a belt that can hold items. She is preparing to do more. She's taking the time to improve herself and her body for the tasks she has ahead of her. She can see hard things coming and knows it's best to prepare and be ready for it.

Takeaway: Hard times will come in this life, be ready to handle them when they do.

Proverbs 31:18 "She perceives that her merchandise *is* good, and her lamp does not go out by night."

Let me say I struggle here. I think that if I made it, then it's not as good as something store-bought. I undervalue my work routinely. But God wants us to feel confident in what He is equipping our hands to do, always giving the glory back to Him.

As for the second part of this verse, the lamp being on all night does not mean she is working all night long. No electricity meant that homes used oil lamps for light. It would be a jar and a wick that you could trim, and it would burn until the oil ran out. What the verse is saying is that the woman remembers to add the oil to her lamp before bed so that it stays on all night. The oil lamp can then be used to see, but also to light other lamps in the early morning, or to light the cooking fire or to assist if danger happens. It's like having your flashlight batteries ready in case something comes up.

Takeaway: She values her work, and she is prepared for the unknown.

Proverbs 31:19 "She stretches out her hands to the distaff, and her hand holds the spindle."

Here is more about how she works with wool and flax. A distaff and spindle are special because they're highly portable. You can do this while chasing toddlers or in between other chores. The distaff would be a longer stick with the wool or flax wound around it loosely in a big fluffy pile. The spindle would be a smaller shaped stick, usually with a weight attached to the end that would dangle and spin as you twisted wool off the distaff. So, she's still working in her main area of homesteading expertise, and what we see with this verse is that she isn't lazy. She uses each moment she can to make things for her family or to sell. Once you have a full spindle you are all set to weave cloth, and as we continue in these verses it's one of the items she sells at the market.

Takeaway: Make the most of your time; use the cracks of life to be productive.

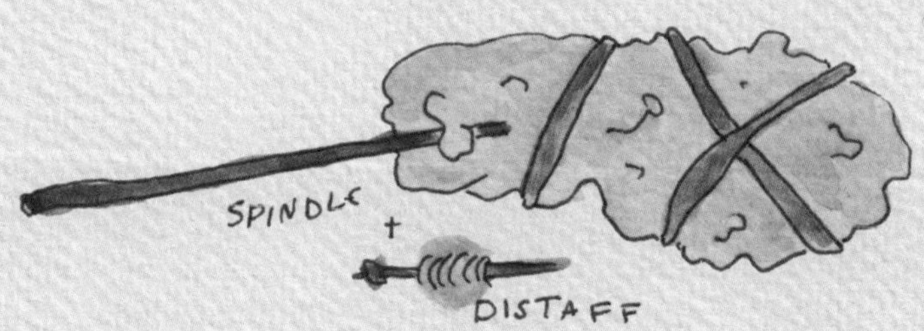

Proverbs 31:2 "She extends her hand to the poor, yes, she reaches out her hands to the needy."

Not only is she providing for her family, but she is helping others. Do you see how work and giving go hand to hand? We are not to be so obsessed with work that we forget those in need.

Takeaway: Don't be over-obsessed with work and storing up money; help the poor, too.

Proverbs 31:21 "She is not afraid of snow for her household, For all her household *is* clothed with scarlet."

It would be very difficult and expensive to get scarlet dye in this era. It would mean she had good relations with merchants from far away, and the color was often reserved for only the wealthy. Can you see the progression of her business and her homestead? The more she leans into what she knows, and the gifts God has given her, the more things are working out. Her family isn't afraid of snow, which means we've had time pass. It's not all at once; it takes time.

Takeaway: Don't assume everything will happen instantly.

Proverbs 31:22 "She makes tapestry for herself; Her clothing *is* fine linen and purple."

Here time has gone by again, and she's becoming an expert in her field. Tapestries are one of the finest forms of wool trade that take many hours, multiple dyed fibers, and some equipment, too. In the same way, linen is the finest form of flax production and is a lightweight fabric that is still used today. Dyeing the linen purple would have required resources (purple dye was expensive) and the technique was difficult to learn.

Takeaway: Keep learning about what God has put before you to do.

Proverbs 31:23 "Her husband is known in the gates, when he sits among the elders of the land."

This may seem strange to read, but gates were a big deal in Bible times. It's the equivalent of going to the capital of your state and seeing all the people in charge. Her husband has access to those in command of her city and could make even more connections because of her good reputation. Because of her years of work and dedication, she now has a reputation that all her family is benefiting from. In our day, this could be a social media presence that glorifies God or a network of business owners who see the value in your products.

Takeaway: We should strive to have a reputation for quality of work and for love of Jesus in our daily lives.

Proverbs 31:24 "She makes linen garments and sells *them,* and supplies sashes for the merchants."

Part of the reason her husband is known is because of all of her activities of selling and making goods for her family and others. She's making clothing fit for royalty because her skills have improved throughout the years, and now it's paying off. She's become the fashion designer of her town in a way, and even more so sells sashes to the merchants. This is significant because a sash was tied at the waist to secure clothing, hold things like a belt, and to designate rank and authority. Basically, the merchants can't do their job unless they have their sashes, and without a sash, commerce would stop.

Takeaway: Others may start relying on your items to keep doing their own work, or you may employ others to keep work going.

Proverbs 31:25 "Strength and honor *are* her clothing; She shall rejoice in time to come."

More time has passed and now she has come to realize something significant; Her worldly treasures and skills are nothing compared to what she has in God. Her clothing, the thing she's an expert at, has left the physical and turned spiritual. It's like most famous or rich people will tell you—money can't buy happiness. God is the source of joy. That's why she is rejoicing in the future. She knows where her hope is, and it's not part of this world.

Takeaway: Deep joy comes from God and not from the things in this world.

Proverbs 31:26 "She opens her mouth with wisdom, and on her tongue *is* the law of kindness."

At this point she has mastered her homestead and is passing on her wisdom to others. She's teaching and being kind. She wants the next generation to learn from her and honor God in the process.

Takeaway: Teaching is a great way to keep the momentum going on our walk with the Lord.

Proverbs 31:27 "She watches over the ways of her household, and does not eat the bread of idleness."

Now that she has taught her children or whomever about how to run her homestead, she keeps watching to be sure things don't go wrong. She is still active, still helping, and giving encouragement to those in her home. Even if she isn't doing everything anymore, it's still a role of guidance and understanding.

Takeaway: When you've mastered a craft, it's important to follow teaching with supervision and guidance.

Proverbs 31:28–29 "Her children rise up and call her blessed; Her husband *also*, and he praises her: 'Many daughters have done well, But you excel them all.'"

I love this testimony from her family. They appreciate her deeply and see the value she has brought to the family. It's an attitude of gratitude which they would have learned from their parents. They aren't freeloading and sitting back while she does it all—they are all in on this family adventure together.

It's a beautiful example of how a family builds each other up in love, encouragement, and hard work.

Takeaway: Don't forget to acknowledge hard work when you see it.

Proverbs 31:30 "Charm *is* deceitful and beauty *is* passing, but a woman *who* fears the Lord, she shall be praised."

This woman has gone her whole life now fearing the Lord. She has seen her physical beauty fade and knows what truly holds value over time. It's something so easily missed in our world of face filters and insta perfect profiles. How we live our lives and what we do has eternal consequences, and if we don't love God with all our hearts, souls, and minds then we will be in big trouble later on as we see our creator face to face.

Takeaway: Remember that the physical is fading but the spiritual is eternal.

Proverbs 31:31 "Give her of the fruit of her hands, And let her own works praise her in the gates."

In ancient times it was often hard for a woman to get paid or to receive praise. The society of the time saw women as less than or even as property of their husbands. When King Lemuel wrote this portion of Proverbs, it was completely countercultural. But God has honored women from the beginning of time, and having it said here yet again is testimony to how much God loves women and thinks highly of them.

Takeaway: When we honor God first in all we do, God returns it with praise and gratitude as well.

Now that we understand how the Virtuous Wife used her skills to be the best she could in her field over the course of her life, it's much easier to appreciate all the work she was doing. She didn't do everything; she had a focus. She kept God at the center of her life. She never stopped learning and growing. She cared for her family, and they also cared for her. This sounds like the kind of homestead I want to be a part of. The kind that does not live in fear of tomorrow or in anger at those in charge, but instead extends an open hand to others and experiences the joy of looking ahead at Jesus who is ultimately in control.

I pray this book has helped you find a focus on your homestead and a steady path forward as you navigate all the possibilities that a homestead can have. I pray that joy, love, and compassion fill your home even on the hardest days. I pray Jesus over you, your family, and your home.

Blessings,
Hannah

Pray

Acknowledgments

I'd like to thank so many of you for following along in my homestead adventures but especially my husband, Ben, who is unwavering in his support. I'd also like to thank my agent, Bethany Jett, who took a chance on me, and my editor, Abigail Gehring, who saw the vision for this book. Finally, I know that without God none of this would have been possible. Praise God from whom all blessings flow.

Recipes

Index

T

U

V

W

Y

Notes

Notes

Notes

Notes

Notes